SHIMBA
BIBLE STUDY SERIES

THE DIVINITY OF JESUS

IN THE GOSPEL OF JOHN

Dr. Maxwell Shimba

Printed in the United States of America

SHIMBA
PUBLISHING

TABLE OF CONTENTS

INTRODUCTION

The Divinity of Jesus in the Gospel of John

The Gospel of John stands out among the four Gospels for its profound theological insights and its clear emphasis on the divinity of Jesus Christ. Unlike the Synoptic Gospels (Matthew, Mark, and Luke), which primarily focus on the events of Jesus' life and His teachings, John's Gospel delves deeply into the spiritual and divine nature of Jesus. From its opening verse to its concluding chapter, the Gospel of John presents Jesus not merely as a remarkable teacher or prophet but as the eternal Word made flesh, the Son of God who has existed from the beginning with God and as God.

The Purpose of John's Gospel

John explicitly states the purpose of his Gospel in John 20:30-31: "Jesus performed many other signs in the presence of his disciples, which are not recorded in this book. But these are written that you may believe that Jesus is the Messiah, the Son of God, and that by believing you may have life in his name." This purpose statement highlights two key objectives: to lead readers to believe in Jesus as the Messiah and the Son of God and to offer them eternal life through this belief. John's Gospel is thus both an invitation to faith and a theological exploration of who Jesus is.

The Pre-existence and Eternality of Jesus

One of the most striking aspects of John's Gospel is its portrayal of Jesus' pre-existence and eternality. The opening verses (John 1:1-3) declare, "In the beginning was the Word, and the Word was with God, and the Word was God. He was with God in the beginning. Through him all things were made; without him, nothing was made that has been made." These verses unequivocally assert Jesus' divinity, identifying Him as the eternal Word (Logos) who was present at the creation of the world and who participated in the creation itself.

The Incarnation: The Word Made Flesh

John 1:14 continues this profound theological reflection by proclaiming, "The Word became flesh and made his dwelling among us. We have seen his glory, the glory of the one and only Son, who came from the Father, full of grace and truth." This declaration of the incarnation—God becoming human in the person of Jesus Christ—underscores the unique nature of Jesus' mission. He is not merely a man anointed by God but God Himself who has entered into human history to reveal His glory and bring salvation to humanity.

The Signs and Miracles

John's Gospel is structured around a series of signs and miracles that reveal Jesus' divine nature. These signs include turning water into wine (John 2:1-11), healing the nobleman's son (John 4:46-54), feeding the 5,000 (John 6:1-14), walking on water (John 6:16-21), healing the man born blind (John 9:1-12), and raising Lazarus from the dead (John 11:1-44). Each of these miracles is a testament to Jesus' divine authority and power, illustrating that He is the source of life, the light of the world, and the conqueror of death.

The "I Am" Statements

In addition to the signs and miracles, John's Gospel features a series of "I Am" statements made by Jesus, each of which reveals a different aspect of His divine identity. These statements include "I am the bread of life" (John 6:35), "I am the light of the world" (John 8:12), "I am the door" (John 10:9), "I am the good shepherd" (John 10:11), "I am the resurrection and the life" (John 11:25), "I am the way, the truth, and the life" (John 14:6), and "I am the true vine" (John 15:1). These declarations not only affirm Jesus' divinity but also provide insight into His role in God's plan of salvation.

The Crucifixion and Resurrection

The culmination of John's presentation of Jesus' divinity is found in the events of His crucifixion and resurrection. John 19 details the sacrificial death of Jesus, portraying it as the ultimate act of love and fulfillment of Scripture. Jesus' declaration "It is finished" (John 19:30) signifies the completion of His redemptive work. In John 20, the resurrection of Jesus from the dead provides the ultimate proof of His divine nature, demonstrating His victory over death and His power to grant eternal life to all who believe in Him.

Conclusion

The Gospel of John provides a rich and multifaceted portrait of Jesus Christ, emphasizing His divinity and eternal existence. Through its theological reflections, miraculous signs, and profound teachings, John's Gospel invites readers to a deeper understanding of who Jesus is and calls them to faith in Him as the Messiah and the Son of God. This belief is not just an intellectual assent but a transformative trust that brings eternal life. As we explore the lessons on the divinity of Jesus in the Gospel of John, we are invited to encounter the living Word, to behold His glory, and to experience the fullness of life in His name.

Dr. Maxwell Shimba

Shimba Theological Institute

DR. MAXWELL SHIMBA

CHAPTER 01

THE WORD MADE FLESH

The Gospel of John opens with a profound declaration about the nature of Jesus Christ, identifying Him as the Word (Logos) who existed from the beginning with God and was, in fact, God Himself. This passage is foundational for understanding the divinity of Jesus and His unique relationship with the Father. John 1:1-18 lays the groundwork for the entire Gospel, presenting Jesus as the eternal Word made flesh, full of grace and truth.

The Eternal Word (John 1:1-2)

"In the beginning was the Word, and the Word was with God, and the Word was God. He was in the beginning with God."

From the very first verse, John establishes the eternal existence of Jesus. Unlike other Gospels that start with Jesus' earthly life, John transcends time, asserting that Jesus, as the Word, existed "in the beginning." This phrase echoes the opening words of Genesis, drawing a parallel between the creation account and the new creation inaugurated through Jesus Christ.

The term "Word" (Logos) is rich with meaning. In Greek philosophy, Logos refers to the principle of reason and order in the universe. In Jewish thought, it represents God's spoken word, through which He created and sustains all things. By identifying Jesus as the Logos, John conveys that Jesus is both the divine reason behind the universe and the active agent of creation.

The assertion that "the Word was with God" emphasizes the intimate relationship between Jesus and the Father. It indicates distinct personhood while affirming unity in essence. The climactic statement, "the Word was God," unequivocally declares the deity of Jesus, leaving no room for interpreting Him merely as a created being or lesser divine figure.

The Creator and Sustainer (John 1:3-5)

"All things were made through Him, and without Him, nothing was made that was made. In Him was life, and the life was the light of men. And the light shines in the darkness, and the darkness did not comprehend it."

John further elaborates on the role of Jesus in creation. As the Logos, Jesus is the conduit through which all things came into being. This underscores His omnipotence and preeminence over creation. Nothing exists apart from His creative will and power.

The statement "In Him was life" signifies that Jesus is the source of all life, both physical and spiritual. The life He gives is not merely biological existence but the fullness of life that reflects God's eternal nature. This life is also "the light of men," symbolizing the revelation of God's truth and presence in the world. The light shines in the darkness, representing the invasion of God's kingdom into a world marred by sin and death. Despite the resistance and inability of darkness to overcome it, the light remains triumphant.

The Witness of John the Baptist (John 1:6-8)

"There was a man sent from God, whose name was John. This man came for a witness, to bear witness of the Light, that all through him might believe. He was not that Light, but was sent to bear witness of that Light."

John the Baptist plays a crucial role in the narrative, serving as the forerunner who prepares the way for Jesus. His mission is to testify about the Light, pointing people to Jesus so that they might believe. John the Baptist's role highlights the importance of testimony in God's redemptive plan. His witness validates Jesus' identity and mission, affirming that He is the true Light sent to illuminate every person.

The Rejection and Reception of the Word (John 1:9-13)

"That was the true Light which gives light to every man coming into the world. He was in the world, and the world was made through Him, and the world did not know Him. He came to His own, and His own did not receive Him. But as many as received Him, to them He gave the right to become children of God, to those who believe in His name: who were born, not of blood, nor of the will of the flesh, nor of the will of man, but of God."

Jesus, as the true Light, came into the world He created, yet He was not recognized or received by it. This rejection is particularly poignant among His own people, the Jews, who were awaiting the Messiah. Their failure to recognize Him underscores the tragic reality of spiritual blindness and the pervasive influence of sin.

However, John offers a message of hope: those who receive Jesus and believe in His name are given the right to become children of God. This new birth is not based on a natural descent, human effort, or decision but is a divine act of grace. It highlights the transformative power of faith in Jesus, enabling believers to enter into a familial relationship with God.

The Word Became Flesh (John 1:14)

"And the Word became flesh and dwelt among us, and we beheld His glory, the glory as of the only begotten of the Father, full of grace and truth."

The incarnation is the pinnacle of the prologue's revelation. The eternal Word took on human flesh, entering the realm of human experience and existence. This profound mystery—God becoming man—demonstrates God's immense love and commitment to redeeming humanity.

The phrase "dwelt among us" evokes the imagery of the Tabernacle in the Old Testament, where God's presence resided among His people. Jesus is the ultimate fulfillment of this concept, embodying God's presence in a tangible and accessible way.

John testifies to witnessing Jesus' glory, a glory that reflects His unique relationship with the Father as the only begotten Son. This glory is characterized by grace and truth, qualities that define Jesus' ministry and reveal the nature of God. Grace emphasizes God's unmerited favor and love, while truth underscores His faithfulness and reliability.

The Testimony of John the Baptist (John 1:15)

"John bore witness of Him and cried out, saying, 'This was He of whom I said, "He who comes after me is preferred before me, for He was before me."'"

John the Baptist reaffirms Jesus' preeminence and eternal existence. Despite coming after John in terms of earthly ministry, Jesus surpasses him because He existed before him. This statement reinforces the divine nature of Jesus and His superiority over all human prophets and messengers.

Grace and Truth Through Jesus Christ (John 1:16-18)

"And of His fullness, we have all received, and grace for grace. For the law was given through Moses, but grace and truth came through Jesus Christ. No one has seen God at any time. The only begotten Son, who is in the bosom of the Father, He has declared Him."

In Jesus, believers receive the fullness of God's grace, continually renewed and overflowing. This grace contrasts with the law given through Moses, which, while revealing God's standards, could not provide the means for true redemption and transformation. Jesus embodies and imparts both grace and truth, offering salvation and revealing the true nature of God.

John concludes by affirming that Jesus, the only begotten Son, is uniquely qualified to reveal God to humanity. No one has seen God, but Jesus, who is intimately united with the Father, makes Him known. This declaration confirms that knowing Jesus is the key to knowing God.

Conclusion

The opening chapter of the Gospel of John presents a profound theological exposition of Jesus' divinity. It asserts His eternal existence, creative power, and unique role as the incarnate Word. Through His life, teachings, and sacrificial death, Jesus reveals the fullness of God's grace and truth, inviting all who believe in Him to become children of God. This foundational understanding of Jesus as the divine Word sets the stage for the rest of the Gospel, which continually unveils His divine identity and redemptive mission.

All Things Were Made Through Him

In the opening verses of the Gospel of John, a profound truth is revealed: "All things were made through Him; and without Him, nothing was made that was made" (John 1:3). This verse is pivotal in understanding the divine nature of Jesus Christ. It highlights His role as the Creator and Sustainer of the universe, affirming His deity and preeminence over all creation. This chapter will delve into the implications of this verse, exploring how it underscores Jesus' divine nature and His integral role in the cosmos.

The Preeminence of Christ in Creation

"All things were made through Him..."

John 1:3 declares that all things were made through Jesus, indicating that He is the agent of creation. This statement places Jesus at the very heart of the creative process, affirming that He is not a mere participant but the divine source through whom everything came into existence. This echoes the creation account in Genesis, where God's spoken word brings the universe into being. By identifying Jesus as the Logos (Word), John asserts that Jesus is the divine Word spoken at creation.

In Colossians 1:16, the Apostle Paul reinforces this truth: "For by Him all things were created that are in heaven and that are on earth, visible and invisible, whether thrones or dominions or principalities or powers. All things were created through Him and for Him." This verse expands on John's declaration, emphasizing that Jesus is the Creator of everything, both seen and unseen. His creative power extends to the entire cosmos, from the smallest atom to the vast galaxies, as well as spiritual realms and authorities.

The Sustainer of All Things

"...without Him, nothing was made that was made."

The latter part of John 1:3 underscores the absolute dependence of all creation on Jesus. Without Him, nothing was made that exists. This statement affirms that Jesus is not only the Creator but also the Sustainer of all things. Everything owes its existence to Him, and nothing can exist apart from His sustaining power.

Hebrews 1:3 speaks to this sustaining role: "Who being the brightness of His glory and the express image of His person, and upholding all things by the word of His power, when He had by Himself purged our sins, sat down at the right hand of the Majesty on high." Jesus upholds the universe by His powerful word, maintaining the order and function of all creation. This continuous act of sustaining the universe is a testament to His divine nature and authority.

The Divine Nature of Jesus

The Eternal Word

The concept of Jesus as the Logos, or Word, is central to understanding His divine nature. In Greek philosophy, Logos signifies the rational principle that governs the universe. In Jewish thought, it represents God's active word in creation and revelation. By identifying Jesus as the Logos, John bridges these concepts, presenting Jesus as the divine reason and the agent through whom God created and sustains the world.

John 1:1-2 establishes Jesus' eternal nature: "In the beginning was the Word, and the Word was with God, and the Word was God. He was in the beginning with God." These verses affirm that Jesus existed before creation, co-eternal with God the Father. He is not a created being but the eternal Word who has always been with God and is Himself,

God. This eternal existence is a hallmark of His divine nature, distinguishing Him from all created beings.

The Incarnation: The Word Became Flesh

John 1:14

The divine nature of Jesus is further revealed in the incarnation: "And the Word became flesh and dwelt among us, and we beheld His glory, the glory as of the only begotten of the Father, full of grace and truth." The eternal Word took on human flesh, entering the realm of human experience. This profound mystery—God becoming man—demonstrates the fullness of Jesus' divine nature.

The incarnation does not diminish Jesus' divinity; rather, it reveals the depth of God's love and His commitment to redeeming humanity. Jesus, fully God and fully man, bridges the gap between the divine and human, providing a way for humanity to be reconciled with God. This dual nature of Jesus—His divinity and humanity—is central to Christian theology and the understanding of His role as Savior.

Jesus is the Image of the Invisible God

Colossians 1:15 describes Jesus as "the image of the invisible God, the firstborn over all creation." As the image of God, Jesus perfectly reveals the nature and character of God the Father. He is the visible representation of the invisible God, making God's attributes and will known to humanity. This revelation is part of His divine nature, as only God can fully reveal Himself.

The term "firstborn over all creation" does not imply that Jesus is a created being but signifies His preeminence and authority over all creation. In Jewish culture, the firstborn held a position of honor and authority. By calling Jesus the firstborn, Paul emphasizes His supreme status and His rightful place as Lord over all creation.

The Implications of Jesus' Divine Nature

Worship and Obedience

Recognizing Jesus as the Creator and Sustainer of all things calls for worship and obedience. His divine nature demands reverence and submission. As the one through whom all things were made, Jesus is worthy of all honor and praise. Revelation 4:11 captures this truth: "You are worthy, O Lord, to receive glory and honor and power; for You created all things, and by Your will they exist and were created."

Assurance of Salvation

Jesus' divine nature also assures believers of the efficacy of His redemptive work. As fully God, Jesus' sacrifice on the cross is of infinite value, sufficient to atone for the sins of the whole world. His resurrection demonstrates His power over death and guarantees eternal life for those who believe in Him. This assurance is rooted in His divine authority and power.

Conclusion

John 1:3 reveals the profound truth of Jesus' divine nature as the Creator and Sustainer of all things. Through Him, everything came into existence, and without Him, nothing exists. This foundational understanding of Jesus' divinity shapes our perception of His role in the cosmos and His redemptive mission. As the eternal Word, Jesus bridges the gap between the divine and human, revealing God's nature and providing a way for reconciliation. His divine nature calls us to worship, obedience, and assurance in His redemptive work. In recognizing Jesus as the Creator and Sustainer, we acknowledge His supreme authority and honor Him as the eternal Word made flesh.

In Him Was Life, and the Life Was the Light of Men

The opening chapter of the Gospel of John is rich with profound theological insights about the divine nature of Jesus Christ. John 1:4-5 states, "In Him was life, and the life was the light of men. And the light shines in the darkness, and the darkness did not comprehend it." This passage encapsulates the essence of Jesus' divinity by portraying Him as the source of life and light for humanity. In this chapter, we will delve into the deep implications of these verses, exploring how they reveal Jesus' divine nature and His role in bringing life and light to the world.

Jesus as the Source of Life

"In Him was life..."

The declaration that "In Him was life" emphasizes that Jesus is the ultimate source of all life. This statement is foundational for understanding His divine nature. Life, in this context, is not merely biological existence but encompasses spiritual and eternal life. It signifies the fullness of life that only God can give.

In the Old Testament, God is often depicted as the source of life. For instance, Psalm 36:9 states, "For with You is the fountain of life; in Your light we see light." By attributing life to Jesus, John aligns Him with the divine identity of God, underscoring His deity. Jesus Himself confirms this in John 14:6, where He declares, "I am the way, the truth, and the life. No one comes to the Father except through Me." This assertion not only highlights His unique role in salvation but also affirms His inherent life-giving power.

The Life-Giver in Creation and Redemption

Jesus' role as the source of life is evident in both creation and redemption. In the creation narrative, God's breath brings life to humanity (Genesis 2:7). Similarly, John 1:3-4 reveals that all creation came into being through Jesus, who imparts life to all living things. This creative power is a hallmark of His divine nature.

In the realm of redemption, Jesus' life-giving power is manifested through His death and resurrection. In John 10:10, Jesus states, "I have come that they may have life, and that they may have it more abundantly." Through His sacrificial death on the cross and His victorious resurrection, Jesus conquers sin and death, offering eternal life to all who believe in Him. This redemptive work is the ultimate expression of His divine nature and His love for humanity.

Jesus as the Light of Men

"...and the life was the light of men."

The second part of John 1:4, "and the life was the light of men," further elaborates on Jesus' divine nature. Light, in biblical symbolism, often represents truth, holiness, and the revelation of God's presence. By describing Jesus as the light of men, John emphasizes that Jesus is the source of divine illumination, guiding humanity out of spiritual darkness and into the truth of God's kingdom.

The Light in Creation and Revelation

The concept of light is deeply rooted in the biblical narrative. In Genesis 1:3, God's first creative act is to speak light into existence: "Then God said, 'Let there be light'; and there was light." This primordial light is a symbol of God's presence and the order He brings to chaos. By identifying Jesus as the light, John connects Him to this creative and revelatory act of God, affirming His divine authority and purpose.

In John 8:12, Jesus proclaims, "I am the light of the world. He who follows Me shall not walk in darkness but have the light of life." This statement highlights Jesus' role in revealing God's truth and dispelling the darkness of sin and ignorance. His teachings, miracles, and very presence embody the light of divine revelation, making God's nature and will known to humanity.

The Light Shines in the Darkness

"And the light shines in the darkness, and the darkness did not comprehend it."

John 1:5 introduces a powerful metaphor of light shining in the darkness. This imagery conveys the ongoing struggle between good and evil, truth and falsehood, life and death. The darkness represents the sinful, fallen state of the world, as opposed to the light of God's truth and holiness.

The Inextinguishable Light

The phrase "the light shines in the darkness" is in the present tense, indicating a continuous action. It signifies that Jesus' light persistently illuminates the darkness, offering hope and redemption. The subsequent statement, "and the darkness did not comprehend it," can also be translated as "the darkness did not overcome it." This dual meaning underscores both the ignorance of the world in recognizing Jesus and the ultimate triumph of His light over darkness.

This victory of light over darkness is a central theme in John's Gospel. Jesus' crucifixion, seemingly a moment of darkness, culminates in the resurrection, the ultimate demonstration of light overcoming darkness. This triumph is a testament to Jesus' divine power and His mission to bring salvation to the world.

The Divine Nature of Jesus as Light and Life

The Self-Existence of Jesus

The declarations that Jesus is the source of life and the light of men reveal His self-existence, a key attribute of divinity. Unlike created beings who derive their life from external sources, Jesus possesses life inherently. This self-existence is an essential characteristic of God, as seen in Exodus 3:14, where God reveals Himself to Moses as "I AM WHO I AM." By ascribing life and light to Jesus, John affirms His co-equality with God the Father.

The Transformative Power of Jesus

Jesus' divine nature as the source of life and light has profound implications for believers. As the life-giver, Jesus offers not only physical existence but also spiritual renewal and eternal life. Believers are called to experience this abundant life through faith in Him. As the light of men, Jesus illuminates the path to righteousness, guiding believers in truth and revealing God's will.

The transformative power of Jesus is evident in the lives of those who follow Him. In 2 Corinthians 5:17, Paul writes, "Therefore, if anyone is in Christ, he is a new creation; old things have passed away; behold, all things have become new." This new creation is a result of the life and light that Jesus imparts, bringing believers into a restored relationship with God.

Conclusion

John 1:4-5 encapsulates the divine nature of Jesus by presenting Him as the source of life and the light of men. These verses reveal that Jesus is not merely a historical figure or a moral teacher but the eternal Word who imparts life and illuminates the truth of God. His life-giving power and His role as the light of the world affirm His deity and His mission to redeem humanity.

As the light shines in the darkness and the darkness cannot overcome it, believers are called to embrace the life and light that Jesus offers. This call invites a transformative relationship with Him, one that brings eternal life and the revelation of God's truth. In recognizing Jesus as the divine source of life and light, we are drawn into a deeper understanding of His nature and His redemptive work, leading us to worship, follow, and share His light with the world.

The Word Became Flesh and Dwelt Among Us

John 1:14 is one of the most profound verses in the Bible, encapsulating the mystery and majesty of the incarnation: "The Word became flesh and dwelt among us, full of grace and truth." This verse is central to understanding the divine nature of Jesus Christ, as it reveals how the eternal Word, who is God, took on human flesh and lived among humanity. In this chapter, we will explore the implications of this verse, delving into the significance of the Word becoming flesh and the manifestation of grace and truth in Jesus.

The Word Became Flesh

The Eternal Word

The opening of John's Gospel introduces Jesus as the Word (Logos), establishing His preexistence and divine nature: "In the beginning was the Word, and the Word was with God, and the Word was God" (John 1:1). The term Logos was rich with meaning in both Greek philosophy and Jewish thought, symbolizing divine reason, order, and creative power. By identifying Jesus as the Logos, John asserts that Jesus is both the agent of creation and the ultimate revelation of God.

The Incarnation

"The Word became flesh" is a declaration of the incarnation, the momentous event where the eternal, divine Word took on human nature. This act of becoming flesh signifies that Jesus, while remaining fully God, also became fully human. The incarnation is a unique and unparalleled event in the history of the world, where God entered into the human experience.

The Apostle Paul echoes this mystery in Philippians 2:6-7: "Who, being in the form of God, did not consider it robbery to be equal with God, but made Himself of no reputation, taking the form of a bondservant, and coming in the likeness of men." Jesus, though equal to God, humbled Himself by becoming a man, demonstrating the depth of His love and the extent of His willingness to redeem humanity.

Dwelt Among Us

God With Us

The phrase "dwelt among us" translates into a Greek term that literally means "pitched His tent" or "tabernacled" among us. This imagery is significant, as it recalls the Old Testament Tabernacle where God's presence dwelled among the Israelites during their journey through the wilderness. In the same way, Jesus, the Word made flesh, is the ultimate fulfillment of God's desire to dwell among His people.

The concept of God dwelling among His people is a recurring theme in Scripture. In the Old Testament, God's presence was manifest in the Tabernacle and later in the temple. However, these were mere shadows of the ultimate reality fulfilled in Jesus. As Emmanuel, "God with us" (Matthew 1:23), Jesus embodies God's presence in a direct and personal way. Through Him, humanity can encounter God not as a distant deity but as a loving and accessible Savior.

The Glory of God Revealed

John continues, "And we beheld His glory, the glory as of the only begotten of the Father." The incarnation allows us to see the glory of God in the person of Jesus Christ. This glory is not merely a radiant display but the manifestation of God's character and nature. Jesus' life, teachings, miracles, death, and resurrection all reveal the divine glory.

In the Old Testament, Moses asked to see God's glory, and God responded that no one could see His face and live (Exodus 33:18-20). Yet, in Jesus, the fullness of God's glory is revealed in a way that humanity can behold. As the only begotten Son, Jesus uniquely reflects the Father's glory, providing a clear and tangible revelation of God's character.

Full of Grace and Truth

The Grace of God

Jesus is described as being "full of grace." Grace is the unmerited favor of God, His love and kindness extended to undeserving humanity. Throughout His ministry, Jesus exemplified grace in His interactions with people. He showed compassion to the sick, the sinner, and the outcast, offering forgiveness and healing without condition.

One of the most poignant examples of Jesus' grace is His encounter with the woman caught in adultery (John 8:1-11). Despite the legalistic demands for her punishment, Jesus extends grace, saying, "Neither do I condemn you; go and sin no more." This act of grace not only forgives her sin but empowers her to live a transformed life.

The ultimate expression of Jesus' grace is seen in His sacrificial death on the cross. Paul writes in Ephesians 2:8-9, "For by grace you have been saved through faith, and that not of yourselves; it is the gift of God, not of works, lest anyone should boast." Jesus' grace provides the way of salvation, reconciling humanity to God and offering eternal life.

The Truth of God

Jesus is also described as being "full of truth." In a world marred by deception and falsehood, Jesus embodies the absolute truth of God. He declares in John 14:6, "I am the way, the truth, and the life. No one comes to the Father except through Me." This claim to be the truth is exclusive and definitive, affirming that a true understanding of God and His will can only be found in Jesus.

Throughout His ministry, Jesus taught the truth about God's kingdom, correcting misconceptions and revealing the deeper realities of God's purposes. His teachings, such as the Sermon on the Mount, provide profound insights into the nature of God's righteousness and the ethical demands of His kingdom.

Moreover, Jesus' life was a living testimony to the truth. He lived a sinless life, perfectly embodying God's commandments and demonstrating the truth of God's love and holiness. His resurrection from the dead is the ultimate vindication of His truth claims, proving His divine authority and the truth of His message.

The Intersection of Grace and Truth

In Jesus, grace and truth are perfectly united. This balance is essential for understanding His divine nature and mission. Grace without truth can lead to permissiveness and a disregard for God's holiness, while truth without grace can result in legalism and condemnation. Jesus embodies both, offering grace that transforms and truth that liberates.

John 1:16-17 further emphasizes this: "And of His fullness we have all received, and grace for grace. For the law was given through Moses, but grace and truth came through Jesus Christ." The law, given through Moses, revealed God's standards but also highlighted humanity's inability to meet them. Jesus, however, brings the fullness of God's grace and truth, providing the means for salvation and the revelation of God's true nature.

The Divine Nature of Jesus in the Incarnation

The Humility of God

The incarnation reveals the profound humility of God. In Philippians 2:8, Paul writes, "And being found in appearance as a man, He humbled Himself and became obedient to the point of death, even the death of the cross." Jesus' willingness to become human and endure suffering and death demonstrates the depth of God's love and His commitment to redeeming humanity.

This humility is also seen in Jesus' life of service. In John 13:1-17, Jesus washes His disciples' feet, an act of humility and service that exemplifies His teachings about greatness in God's kingdom. Through His actions, Jesus reveals that true greatness is found in serving others, reflecting the self-giving love of God.

The Revelation of God

The incarnation also reveals God's desire to be known by His creation. Throughout history, God has communicated with humanity through various means, including prophets, scriptures, and divine interventions. In Jesus, however, God provides the ultimate revelation of Himself. Hebrews 1:1-2 states, "God, who at various times and in various ways spoke in time past to the fathers by the prophets, has in these last days spoken to us by His Son."

Jesus' life and teachings are the clearest and most direct revelation of God's character, will, and purposes. Through Him, we see the fullness of God's grace and truth, His love and justice, His mercy and holiness. This revelation invites us into a personal relationship with God, grounded in the knowledge of who He is as revealed in Jesus Christ.

Conclusion

John 1:14 encapsulates the mystery and majesty of the incarnation, revealing the divine nature of Jesus Christ. The eternal Word becoming flesh and dwelling among us is the ultimate expression of God's love and His desire to redeem and restore humanity. In Jesus, we behold the glory of God, full of grace and truth, inviting us to experience His life-transforming power.

As we contemplate the profound truths of this verse, we are drawn into a deeper understanding of who Jesus is and what He has accomplished. His incarnation calls us to worship, follow, and share the good news of His grace and truth with the world. Through Him, we encounter the fullness of God's love and the revelation of His divine nature, leading us into a life of faith, hope, and eternal fellowship with God.

No One Has Ever Seen God

John 1:18 (NIV) states, "No one has ever seen God, but the one and only Son, who is himself God and is in closest relationship with the Father, has made him known." This verse is profound in its declaration of Jesus' divine nature and His unique role in revealing God to humanity. It encapsulates the mystery of the incarnation and the intimate relationship between the Father and the Son. In this chapter, we will delve into the implications of this verse, exploring how it reveals Jesus' divine nature and His mission to make God known.

The Invisibility of God

"No one has ever seen God..."

The assertion that no one has ever seen God highlights the fundamental truth about God's nature: His invisibility and transcendence. Throughout the Old Testament, God is depicted as dwelling in unapproachable light, unseen by human eyes. Exodus 33:20 states, "But," he said, "you cannot see my face, for no one may see me and live." This emphasizes the holiness and majesty of God, who is beyond the capacity of human perception.

The invisibility of God underscores the need for a mediator, someone who can bridge the gap between the divine and human. This sets the stage for the revelation of Jesus Christ, the one who makes the invisible God known to humanity.

The Unique Revelation of the Son

"...but the one and only Son, who is himself God and is in closest relationship with the Father..."

This part of the verse introduces the unique status of Jesus as the "one and only Son," affirming His deity and His intimate relationship with the Father. The phrase "who is himself God" leaves no ambiguity about Jesus' divine nature. He is not merely a prophet or a teacher but God incarnate.

The term "one and only" (Greek: monogenes) signifies Jesus' unique and singular nature. He is the only Son of God in a way that no other being is. This uniqueness is further emphasized by His relationship with the Father, described as "in closest relationship with the Father" (Greek: eis ton kolpon tou Patros), literally meaning "in the bosom of the Father." This imagery conveys an intimate and eternal bond between the Father and the Son, highlighting their unity and mutual love.

Making God Known

"...has made him known."

The climax of the verse is the declaration that Jesus "has made him known." The Greek word used here, exegesato, from which we get the word "exegesis," means to explain, interpret, or reveal. Jesus, as the divine Son, interprets and reveals the Father to humanity. He is the ultimate revelation of God, making the invisible God visible and accessible.

The Role of Jesus in Revelation

The Incarnation as Revelation

The incarnation is the definitive act of revelation. When "the Word became flesh" (John 1:14), God's nature and character were fully revealed in Jesus Christ. Through His life, teachings, miracles, death, and resurrection, Jesus provides a clear and comprehensive picture of who God is. Hebrews 1:3 states, "The Son is the radiance of God's glory and the exact representation of his being, sustaining all things by his powerful word." This affirms that Jesus perfectly reflects God's glory and nature, making Him the ultimate revelation of God.

The Teachings of Jesus

Throughout His ministry, Jesus consistently pointed to His unique relationship with the Father and His role in revealing Him. In John 14:9, Jesus says to Philip, "Anyone who has seen me has seen the Father." This bold statement underscores that to know Jesus is to know God. His teachings about God's kingdom, love, justice, and mercy are direct revelations of the Father's heart and will.

The Miracles of Jesus

The miracles performed by Jesus also serve as a revelation of God's nature. They demonstrate His power, compassion, and authority. For instance, when Jesus heals the sick, raises the dead, and forgives sins, He reveals God's desire for restoration and wholeness. These acts are not just displays of power but signs pointing to the reality of God's kingdom breaking into the world.

The Divine Nature of Jesus

Unity with the Father

The close relationship between Jesus and the Father is central to understanding His divine nature. In John 10:30, Jesus declares, "I and the Father are one." This unity is not merely a unity of purpose but of essence. Jesus shares in the very nature of God, making Him fully divine. This unity is foundational to His ability to reveal God perfectly.

Preexistence and Eternity

The preexistence of Jesus is another key aspect of His divine nature. John 1:1-2 states, "In the beginning was the Word, and the Word was with God, and the Word was God. He was with God in the beginning." Jesus exists from eternity, co-equal and co-eternal with the Father. This eternal existence distinguishes Him from all created beings and affirms His deity.

The Role of the Holy Spirit

The Holy Spirit also plays a vital role in the revelation of Jesus and, consequently, the revelation of the Father. Jesus promises the coming of the Spirit who will guide believers into all truth (John 16:13). The Spirit continues the work of revelation, helping believers understand and experience the fullness of God's nature as revealed in Jesus Christ.

The Implications for Believers

Knowing God Through Jesus

The revelation of God through Jesus has profound implications for believers. It means that the true knowledge of God is found in a personal relationship with Jesus Christ. Through Him, we have access to the Father and can experience His love, grace, and truth. This relationship is the foundation of the Christian faith, providing the assurance of salvation and the hope of eternal life.

The Call to Reflect God's Nature

As followers of Jesus, believers are called to reflect God's nature as revealed in Christ. This involves living lives marked by grace and truth, embodying the love and holiness of God in our interactions with others. The revelation of God in Jesus is not only a theological truth to be affirmed but a transformative reality to be lived out in daily life.

Conclusion

John 1:18 (NIV) encapsulates the profound mystery and majesty of Jesus' divine nature and His unique role in revealing God to humanity. As the one and only Son who is Himself God and in closest relationship with the Father, Jesus makes the invisible God known. Through His incarnation, teachings, miracles, and the ongoing work of the Holy Spirit, Jesus provides the ultimate revelation of God's character and will.

Understanding Jesus as the full revelation of God invites us into a deeper relationship with Him, transforming our lives and calling us to reflect His grace and truth in the world. In knowing Jesus, we come to know the Father, experiencing the fullness of His love and the power of His redemptive work. This foundational truth is at the heart of the Christian faith, shaping our understanding of God and our identity as His children.

Jesus is the Bridge Between Heaven and Earth

The concept of Jesus as the bridge between heaven and earth is beautifully encapsulated in John 1:51. This imagery not only highlights Jesus' unique role as the mediator between God and humanity but also reflects the fulfillment of various Old Testament symbols and prophecies. This chapter explores the significance of Jesus as the bridge, focusing on John 1:51, and delves into how this understanding enriches our comprehension of His divine mission.

Jesus' Declaration in John 1:51

John 1:51 (NIV): "He then added, 'Very truly I tell you, you will see heaven open, and the angels of God ascending and descending on the Son of Man.'"

Context and Analysis

1. Context: Jesus speaks these words to Nathanael, one of His early disciples, who is amazed by Jesus' supernatural knowledge about him.

2. Angels Ascending and Descending: This imagery recalls Jacob's dream in Genesis 28:12, where he saw a ladder

reaching to heaven with angels ascending and descending on it.

3. Son of Man: Jesus uses the title "Son of Man," which emphasizes His role as the Messiah and His connection to humanity.

Strong's Concordance Insights:

- Ascending (ἀναβαίνω, anabaino, Strong's G305): To go up, ascend.

- Descending (καταβαίνω, katabaino, Strong's G2597): To come down, descend.

- Son of Man (ὁ υἱὸς τοῦ ἀνθρώπου, ho huios tou anthrōpou, Strong's G5207 and G444): A title Jesus used for Himself, emphasizing His humanity and messianic role.

The Significance of Jesus as the Bridge

1. Mediator Between God and Humanity:

1 Timothy 2:5 (NIV): "For there is one God and one mediator between God and mankind, the man Christ Jesus."

- Explanation: Jesus is the sole mediator who bridges the gap between a holy God and sinful humanity. His life, death, and resurrection enable direct access to God.

2. Fulfillment of Jacob's Ladder:

Genesis 28:12 (NIV): "He had a dream in which he saw a stairway resting on the earth, with its top reaching to heaven, and the angels of God were ascending and descending on it."

- Explanation: Jacob's ladder symbolizes the connection between heaven and earth. Jesus fulfills this vision, becoming the ultimate means of connection between God and humanity.

3. Access to God's Presence:

Ephesians 2:18 (NIV): "For through him we both have access to the Father by one Spirit."

- Explanation: Jesus provides believers with direct access to the Father, breaking down the barriers that separated humanity from God.

4. The Revelation of God's Glory:

John 1:14 (NIV): "The Word became flesh and made his dwelling among us. We have seen his glory, the glory of the one and only Son, who came from the Father, full of grace and truth."

- Explanation: Jesus, as the Word made flesh, reveals God's glory and brings divine grace and truth to humanity.

Theological Implications

1. Incarnation and Revelation:

- Incarnation: Jesus, as God incarnate, embodies the divine presence on earth. He is the tangible manifestation of God's glory and love.

- Revelation: Through Jesus, God reveals His character, will, and redemptive plan.

2. Redemption and Reconciliation:

- Redemption: Jesus' sacrificial death redeems humanity from sin, fulfilling the requirements of divine justice.

- Reconciliation: Through Jesus, humanity is reconciled to God, restoring the broken relationship caused by sin.

2 Corinthians 5:18-19 (NIV):

18 All this is from God, who reconciled us to himself through Christ and gave us the ministry of reconciliation:

19 that God was reconciling the world to himself in Christ, not counting people's sins against them. And he has committed to us the message of reconciliation.

- Explanation: Jesus' work of reconciliation brings peace between God and humanity, allowing believers to become ambassadors of this reconciliation.

3. New Covenant:

- Explanation: Jesus establishes a new covenant through His blood, providing a direct and permanent relationship with God.

Luke 22:20 (NIV): "In the same way, after the supper he took the cup, saying, 'This cup is the new covenant in my blood, which is poured out for you.'"

- Explanation: The new covenant is characterized by grace and truth, fulfilled in Jesus' sacrificial act.

Jesus as the Fulfillment of Old Testament Types

1. The Tabernacle and Temple:

- Explanation: Jesus fulfills the function of the Tabernacle and Temple as the dwelling place of God's presence among His people.

John 2:19-21 (NIV):

19 Jesus answered them, "Destroy this temple, and I will raise it again in three days."

20 They replied, "It has taken forty-six years to build this temple, and you are going to raise it in three days?"

21 But the temple he had spoken of was his body.

- Explanation: Jesus' body is the true temple where God's presence dwells and His resurrection signifies the new, eternal temple.

2. The Sacrificial System:

- Explanation: Jesus is the ultimate sacrifice, fulfilling the Old Testament sacrificial system and providing a once-for-all atonement for sin.

Hebrews 10:10 (NIV): "And by that will, we have been made holy through the sacrifice of the body of Jesus Christ once and for all."

- Explanation: Jesus' sacrifice is sufficient to cleanse from sin and bring believers into a holy relationship with God.

3. The High Priest:

- Explanation: Jesus serves as the eternal High Priest, mediating between God and humanity.

Hebrews 4:14-16 (NIV):

14 Therefore, since we have a great high priest who has ascended into heaven, Jesus the Son of God, let us hold firmly to the faith we profess.

15 For we do not have a high priest who is unable to feel sympathy for our weaknesses, but we have one who has been tempted in every way, just as we are—yet he did not sin.

16 Let us then approach God's throne of grace with confidence, so that we may receive mercy and find grace to help us in our time of need.

- Explanation: Jesus' priestly role assures believers of access to God's grace and mercy.

Practical Implications for Believers

1. Assurance of Salvation:

- Explanation: Believers can have confidence in their salvation, knowing that Jesus has secured their relationship with God.

John 10:28-29 (NIV):

28 I give them eternal life, and they shall never perish; no one will snatch them out of my hand.

29 My Father, who has given them to me, is greater than all; no one can snatch them out of my Father's hand.

- Explanation: Jesus' role as the bridge guarantees eternal security for believers.

2. Empowered Prayer Life:

- Explanation: Believers have direct access to God through Jesus, empowering their prayer life.

Hebrews 4:16 (NIV): "Let us then approach God's throne of grace with confidence, so that we may receive mercy and find grace to help us in our time of need."

- Explanation: The confidence to approach God in prayer is grounded in Jesus' mediating work.

3. Mission and Evangelism:

- Explanation: Believers are called to share the message of reconciliation with others, extending the invitation to experience God's grace.

2 Corinthians 5:20 (NIV): "We are therefore Christ's ambassadors, as though God were making his appeal through us. We implore you on Christ's behalf: Be reconciled to God."

- Explanation: As ambassadors of Christ, believers participate in God's mission to reconcile the world to Himself.

Conclusion

Jesus as the bridge between heaven and earth is a profound theological truth that reveals His unique role in God's redemptive plan. Through His life, death, and resurrection, Jesus provides the way for humanity to be reconciled to God, fulfilling the symbolism of Jacob's ladder and numerous Old Testament types. This understanding enriches our comprehension of Jesus' divine mission and its practical implications for believers, offering assurance of salvation, empowering prayer, and motivating mission. By recognizing Jesus as the ultimate mediator, we gain a deeper appreciation of His sacrifice and the access to God's presence that He provides.

CHAPTER 02

JESUS AS THE LIGHT OF THE WORLD

In the Gospel of John, Jesus is portrayed as the true light that gives light to every person coming into the world. John 1:9-13 (NIV) states, "The true light that gives light to everyone was coming into the world. He was in the world, and though the world was made through him, the world did not recognize him. He came to that which was his own, but his own did not receive him. Yet to all who did receive him, to those who believed in his name, he gave the right to become children of God—children born not of natural descent, nor of human decision or a husband's will, but born of God." This chapter delves into the implications of these verses, exploring how they reveal the divine nature of Jesus and His role as the light of the world.

The True Light

"The true light that gives light to everyone was coming into the world."

The declaration that Jesus is the "true light" highlights His unique and unparalleled role in illuminating the spiritual darkness of the world. Light, in biblical symbolism, often represents truth, purity, and the presence of God. By calling Jesus the true light, John affirms that Jesus is the ultimate source of divine truth and revelation.

Throughout the Bible, light is associated with God and His guidance. In the Old Testament, God's word is described as a lamp to guide the way (Psalm 119:105). In the New Testament, Jesus embodies this divine light, bringing clarity, direction, and hope to a world darkened by sin and ignorance. His coming into the world signifies the dawn of a new era where God's truth is fully revealed through Him.

The Rejection of the Light

"He was in the world, and though the world was made through him, the world did not recognize him. He came to that which was his own, but his own did not receive him."

These verses poignantly describe the tragedy of humanity's response to Jesus. Despite being the Creator of the world, Jesus was not recognized by the world He made. This failure to recognize Him underscores the spiritual blindness and hardness of the heart that pervades humanity.

Jesus' rejection by His own people, the Israelites, is particularly tragic. As the chosen people of God, they had been prepared through the law and the prophets to recognize the Messiah. Yet, when the true light came, they did not receive Him. This rejection fulfills the prophecy of Isaiah 53:3, which describes the suffering servant as "despised and rejected by mankind."

The Acceptance of the Light

"Yet to all who did receive him, to those who believed in his name, he gave the right to become children of God."

Despite widespread rejection, there is a profound promise for those who receive and believe in Jesus. To these individuals, Jesus gives them the right to become children of God. This right is not based on natural descent, human decision, or a husband's will, but is a divine gift of grace.

The Divine Nature of Jesus as the Light

The Source of Divine Illumination

Jesus' role as the light of the world underscores His divine nature as the source of all spiritual illumination. In John 8:12, Jesus declares, "I am the light of the world. Whoever follows me will never walk in darkness, but will have the light of life." This statement affirms that Jesus is not only the revealer of God's truth but also the sustainer of spiritual life.

Throughout His ministry, Jesus illuminated the truth of God's kingdom, corrected misconceptions, and revealed the heart of God. His teachings, such as the Sermon on the Mount, provide profound insights into the nature of God's righteousness and the ethical demands of His kingdom. Jesus' miracles also serve as signs of His divine light, demonstrating His power over darkness, disease, and death.

The Revelation of God

As the true light, Jesus reveals the nature and character of God. In John 14:9, He tells Philip, "Anyone who has seen me has seen the Father." This declaration affirms that Jesus is the visible representation of the invisible God. Through His words and actions, Jesus makes known the love, holiness, justice, and mercy of God.

The revelation of God through Jesus is comprehensive and transformative. It goes beyond mere intellectual knowledge to a relational understanding of God's heart. By receiving Jesus and believing in His name, individuals are invited into a personal relationship with God, experiencing His love and grace in a profound way.

Becoming Children of God

The Right to Become Children of God

The promise that those who receive Jesus and believe in His name are given the right to become children of God is one of the most profound aspects of the Gospel. This right is not earned but bestowed by grace through faith. It signifies a radical transformation in identity and status.

As children of God, believers are adopted into God's family, enjoying the privileges and responsibilities that come with this new identity. This includes intimate access to the Father, the assurance of His love, and the inheritance of eternal life. Romans 8:15-17 beautifully captures this reality: "The Spirit you received does not make you slaves, so that you live in fear again; rather, the Spirit you received brought about your adoption to sonship. And by him we cry, 'Abba, Father.' The Spirit himself testifies with our spirit that we are God's children. Now if we are children, then we are heirs—heirs of God and co-heirs with Christ, if indeed we share in his sufferings in order that we may also share in his glory."

Born of God

John emphasizes that this new birth is not of natural descent, human decision, or a husband's will, but born of God. This signifies that becoming a child of God is a supernatural act of divine grace. It is not dependent on human effort or lineage but on God's initiative and power.

The concept of being born of God is further explored in John 3:3-8, where Jesus explains to Nicodemus the necessity of being "born again" to see the kingdom of God.

This spiritual rebirth is effected by the Holy Spirit, who regenerates and renews believers, making them new creations in Christ.

The Implications for Believers

Living in the Light

As recipients of Jesus' light, believers are called to live in the light. This involves walking in the truth, living according to God's commandments, and reflecting His character in the world. Ephesians 5:8-9 exhorts believers, "For you were once darkness, but now you are light in the Lord. Live as children of light (for the fruit of the light consists in all goodness, righteousness, and truth)."

Living in the light also means rejecting the deeds of darkness and exposing them to the light of God's truth. This involves a commitment to holiness, integrity, and justice, as well as a willingness to bear witness to the transformative power of Jesus in our lives.

Sharing the Light

As followers of Jesus, believers are called to share the light with others. This involves proclaiming the Gospel, demonstrating God's love through acts of compassion and service, and bearing witness to the truth of Jesus. Matthew 5:14-16 highlights this responsibility: "You are the light of the world. A town built on a hill cannot be hidden. Neither do people light a lamp and put it under a bowl. Instead, they put it on its stand, and it gives light to everyone in the house. In the same way, let your light shine before others, that they may see your good deeds and glorify your Father in heaven."

Conclusion

John 1:9-13 reveals the profound truth of Jesus' divine nature as the true light of the world. His coming into the world brings the light of God's truth, illuminating the darkness and offering the promise of becoming children of God to all who receive Him and believe in His name. This revelation invites us into a transformative relationship with God, marked by the assurance of His love and the call to live and share His light.

As we embrace Jesus as the true light, we are invited to experience the fullness of God's grace and truth, walking in the light and reflecting His character in the world. This foundational understanding of Jesus' divine nature and mission shapes our identity as believers and empowers us to fulfill our calling as children of God. Through Jesus, we encounter the true light that dispels darkness and leads us into the glorious reality of God's kingdom.

Jesus as the Light of the World

In John 8:12, Jesus makes a profound declaration: "I am the light of the world. Whoever follows me will never walk in darkness but will have the light of life." This statement is central to understanding the divine nature of Jesus and His role in bringing spiritual illumination to humanity. In this chapter, we will delve into the significance of this declaration, exploring how Jesus embodies the light of the world and what it means for those who follow Him.

Jesus as the Light of the World

"I am the light of the world..."

The metaphor of light is powerful and deeply rooted in biblical symbolism. Light represents truth, purity, guidance, and the presence of God. By identifying Himself as the light of the world, Jesus asserts His unique role as the source of divine truth and the one who reveals God's presence to humanity.

In the context of John 8, Jesus' declaration follows the Feast of Tabernacles, a Jewish festival that included the lighting of large lamps in the temple courts to commemorate God's guidance of Israel through the wilderness with a pillar of fire. Jesus positions Himself as the fulfillment of this symbolism, claiming to be the ultimate light that guides humanity out of spiritual darkness.

The Divine Nature of Jesus as Light

The Source of Divine Illumination

As the light of the world, Jesus is the source of all spiritual illumination. This role highlights His divine nature, as only God can provide the ultimate revelation of truth and guide people out of darkness. Throughout His ministry, Jesus' teachings and actions revealed the nature of God, corrected misconceptions and provided a path to righteousness.

In John 1:4-5, we read, "In him was life, and that life was the light of all mankind. The light shines in the darkness, and the darkness has not overcome it." This passage underscores the continuous and victorious nature of Jesus' light. Despite the presence of darkness in the world, the light of Jesus remains unextinguished and triumphant.

The Revelation of God

Jesus' role as the light involves revealing the true nature of God. In John 14:9, Jesus says to Philip, "Anyone who has seen me has seen the Father." This statement affirms that Jesus is the visible representation of the invisible God. Through Him, we see the love, holiness, justice, and mercy of God manifested in tangible ways.

The miracles performed by Jesus also serve as revelations of His divine light. Each miracle not only addresses a physical need but also points to a deeper spiritual truth about God's kingdom. For instance, when Jesus heals the blind man in John 9, He declares, "While I am in the world, I am the light of the world" (John 9:5), signifying that His power to restore physical sight is a sign of His ability to illuminate spiritual blindness.

The Call to Follow the Light

"...Whoever follows me will never walk in darkness but will have the light of life."

The promise that those who follow Jesus will never walk in darkness but will have the light of life is both a profound assurance and a call to discipleship. To follow Jesus means to commit to His teachings, embrace His way of life, and walk in His light.

Walking in the light involves living according to the truth revealed by Jesus. It means rejecting the deeds of darkness—sin, falsehood, and moral compromise—and embracing a life of holiness, integrity, and love. Ephesians 5:8-9 exhorts believers, "For you were once darkness, but now you are light in the Lord. Live as children of light (for the fruit of the light consists in all goodness, righteousness, and truth)."

The Light of Life

Eternal and Abundant Life

The "light of life" that Jesus promises to those who follow Him encompasses both eternal life and abundant life here and now. Eternal life refers to the unending fellowship with God that believers will enjoy after this life. Jesus, through His death and resurrection, conquers sin and death, offering eternal life to all who believe in Him.

Abundant life, as described in John 10:10, "I have come that they may have life, and have it to the full," refers to the quality of life that Jesus offers here and now. It is a life characterized by joy, peace, purpose, and the indwelling presence of God. This abundant life is a foretaste of the eternal life to come and is marked by the light of Jesus guiding and transforming every aspect of our existence.

The Implications for Believers

Living in the Light

Believers are called to live in the light of Jesus. This involves daily aligning our lives with His teachings, allowing His truth to guide our decisions and actions. It means being transparent, honest, and walking in integrity, as 1 John 1:7 encourages, "But if we walk in the light, as he is in the light, we have fellowship with one another, and the blood of Jesus, his Son, purifies us from all sin."

Living in the light also means being a light to others. Jesus calls His followers to reflect His light in the world, as seen in Matthew 5:14-16, "You are the light of the world. A town built on a hill cannot be hidden. Neither do people light a lamp and put it under a bowl. Instead, they put it on its stand, and it gives light to everyone in the house. In the same way, let your light shine before others, that they may see your good deeds and glorify your Father in heaven." Believers are to be witnesses to the transformative power of Jesus, bringing His light to dark places and pointing others to Him.

Conclusion

John 8:12 encapsulates the profound truth of Jesus' divine nature as the light of the world. His declaration, "I am the light of the world. Whoever follows me will never walk in darkness but will have the light of life," invites us to embrace Him as the source of divine illumination and the revealer of God's truth. As we follow Jesus, we are called to walk in His light, experiencing the abundant and eternal life He offers and reflecting His light to the world around us.

Understanding Jesus as the light of the world shapes our identity and mission as believers. It calls us to live in the truth, reject darkness, and bearers of His light in a world that desperately needs it. Through Jesus, we encounter the true light that dispels darkness and leads us into the fullness of God's life and love.

CHAPTER 03

JESUS AND THE FATHER ARE ONE

In John 10:30, Jesus makes a profound and provocative statement: "I and the Father are one." This declaration is central to understanding the divine nature of Jesus and His unique relationship with God the Father. It emphasizes the unity and oneness of Jesus with the Father, revealing His divine identity and authority. In this chapter, we will explore the implications of this statement, delving into the theological depth of Jesus' claim and its significance for believers.

The Context of the Declaration

The Good Shepherd

The context of John 10:30 is Jesus' discourse on being the Good Shepherd. In John 10:11, Jesus says, "I am the good shepherd. The good shepherd lays down his life for the sheep." Throughout this passage, Jesus contrasts Himself with the hired hand who does not care for the sheep. He emphasizes His deep commitment to His flock, willing to sacrifice His life for their well-being.

In John 10:27-29, just before declaring His oneness with the Father, Jesus speaks about His sheep hearing His voice, following Him, and receiving eternal life. He assures them that no one can snatch them out of His hand, and then extends this assurance to the Father's protection: "My Father, who has given them to me, is greater than all; no one can snatch them out of my Father's hand." This sets the stage for His statement of unity with the Father.

The Declaration of Oneness

"I and the Father are one."

When Jesus declares, "I and the Father are one," He is affirming a profound theological truth about His divine nature and relationship with God the Father. This statement underscores several key aspects of His identity:

1. Unity of Essence: Jesus is claiming that He and the Father are one in essence and nature. This goes beyond mere agreement or harmony; it speaks to a shared divine substance. Jesus is affirming that He is fully God, co-equal with the Father in all aspects of His being.

2. Unity of Purpose: Jesus' mission is in complete alignment with the Father's will. Throughout His ministry,

Jesus repeatedly emphasizes that He came to do the Father's will (John 6:38). Their unity is demonstrated in their shared purpose of salvation and the protection of believers.

3. Divine Authority: By claiming oneness with the Father, Jesus is asserting His divine authority. This authority is evident in His power to grant eternal life and protect His sheep from any force that might seek to harm them.

The Reaction of the Jewish Leaders

Hostility and Accusations

The Jewish leaders' reaction to Jesus' declaration reveals the gravity of His claim. In John 10:31-33, we read, "Again his Jewish opponents picked up stones to stone him, but Jesus said to them, 'I have shown you many good works from the Father. For which of these do you stone me?' 'We are not stoning you for any good work,' they replied, 'but for blasphemy, because you, a mere man, claim to be God.'"

The leaders understood that Jesus was claiming equality with God, which they considered blasphemy. Their intent to stone Him underscores the seriousness with which they viewed His statement. This reaction also highlights the radical nature of Jesus' identity and mission, which challenged the established religious norms and expectations.

Theological Implications of Oneness

The Trinity

Jesus' declaration of oneness with the Father is foundational to the Christian doctrine of the Trinity. The Trinity is the belief in one God who exists in three distinct persons: the Father, the Son (Jesus Christ), and the Holy Spirit. Each person is fully God, sharing the same divine essence, yet distinct in their personhood and roles.

The concept of the Trinity is a mystery that transcends human understanding, but it is essential for grasping the full revelation of God's nature. Jesus' claim to be one with the Father affirms His place within the Trinity and underscores the unity and diversity within the Godhead.

Revelation of God's Nature

Through His unity with the Father, Jesus reveals the nature and character of God. In John 14:9, Jesus tells Philip, "Anyone who has seen me has seen the Father." This statement underscores that Jesus' life, teachings, and actions are the perfect representation of God's nature. In Him, we see God's love, compassion, holiness, and truth made manifest.

This revelation invites believers into a deeper relationship with God. By knowing Jesus, we come to know the Father more intimately. Jesus bridges the gap between the divine and human, providing a way for us to experience the fullness of God's presence and love.

The Assurance for Believers

Eternal Security

Jesus' unity with the Father provides profound assurance for believers. In John 10:28-29, He promises eternal security for His sheep: "I give them eternal life, and they shall never perish; no one will snatch them out of my hand. My Father, who has given them to me, is greater than all; no one can snatch them out of my Father's hand."

This assurance is rooted in the divine power and faithfulness of both the Father and the Son. Believers can trust in their eternal security, knowing that their salvation is upheld by the omnipotent God. This promise is a source of comfort and strength, especially in times of trial and uncertainty.

Unity in the Body of Christ

Jesus' unity with the Father also has implications for the unity of His followers. In His high priestly prayer, Jesus prays for the unity of believers: "I pray also for those who will believe in me through their message, that all of them may be one, Father, just as you are in me and I am in you" (John 17:20-21).

This prayer underscores the importance of unity within the body of Christ. As believers, we are called to reflect the unity of the Father and the Son in our relationships with one another. This unity is a powerful testimony to the world of God's love and the truth of the Gospel.

Conclusion

John 10:30 encapsulates a profound truth about Jesus' divine nature and His unique relationship with the Father: "I and the Father are one." This statement reveals the unity of essence, purpose, and authority between Jesus and the Father, affirming His deity and His role within the Trinity.

Understanding Jesus' oneness with the Father deepens our appreciation of His mission and the assurance He provides to believers. It invites us into a transformative relationship with God, where we experience His love, security, and unity. As we follow Jesus, we are called to reflect His unity with the Father in our lives, demonstrating the reality of His divine nature to the world.

This foundational truth shapes our identity and mission as followers of Christ, empowering us to live in the light of His presence and to share the hope and love of the Gospel with others. Through Jesus, we encounter the fullness of God's revelation, experiencing the profound reality of His oneness and the transformative power of His love.

Jesus and the Father Are One

In John 14:9-11, Jesus makes a profound statement that affirms His divine identity and unity with God the Father:

"Jesus answered: 'Don't you know me, Philip, even after I have been among you such a long time? Anyone who has seen me has seen the Father. How can you say, 'Show us the Father'? Don't you believe that I am in the Father, and that the Father is in me? The words I say to you I do not speak on my own authority. Rather, it is the Father, living in me, who is doing his work. Believe me when I say that I am in the Father and the Father is in me; or at least believe on the evidence of the works themselves.'" This passage provides a clear and compelling insight into the divine nature of Jesus and His intimate relationship with the Father. In this chapter, we will delve into the significance of Jesus' words, exploring how they reveal His divine identity and unity with God.

The Context of Jesus' Declaration

The Upper Room Discourse

The setting of John 14 is the Upper Room, where Jesus is sharing a final meal with His disciples before His arrest and crucifixion. This section of John's Gospel, often referred to as the Upper Room Discourse, contains some of Jesus' most intimate and profound teachings. It is here that He seeks to prepare His disciples for the coming trials and to reassure them of His continuing presence and guidance.

Philip's Request

In John 14:8, Philip makes a request: "Lord, show us the Father and that will be enough for us." This request reflects a deep longing to see and know God more fully. Jesus' response to Philip's request forms the basis of His profound declaration about His unity with the Father.

Jesus Reveals the Father

"Anyone who has seen me has seen the Father."

Jesus' statement, "Anyone who has seen me has seen the Father," is a direct assertion of His divine identity. He is not merely a representative of God or a prophet; He is the exact representation of God. This claim underscores that Jesus embodies the fullness of God's nature and character. To see Jesus is to see God Himself.

In Colossians 1:15, the Apostle Paul echoes this truth: "The Son is the image of the invisible God, the firstborn over all creation." Jesus makes the invisible God visible, revealing God's love, holiness, compassion, and truth in a way that is accessible and comprehensible to humanity.

The Unity of Jesus and the Father

Jesus continues, "Don't you believe that I am in the Father, and that the Father is in me?" This rhetorical question emphasizes the profound unity between Jesus and the Father. Their relationship is characterized by mutual indwelling, where Jesus is in the Father and the Father is in Jesus. This unity goes beyond a mere agreement of purpose or mission; it speaks to an essential oneness in their divine nature.

This mutual indwelling is a mystery that points to the doctrine of the Trinity, where the Father, Son, and Holy Spirit are distinct persons yet one in essence. The unity between Jesus and the Father highlights the co-equality and co-eternity of the Son with the Father, affirming His full divinity.

The Authority and Works of Jesus

"The words I say to you I do not speak on my own authority. Rather, it is the Father, living in me, who is doing his work."

Jesus explains that His words and works are not done on His own authority but are a direct expression of the Father's will and power. This statement underscores the intimate cooperation and harmony between Jesus and the Father. Every word Jesus speaks and every miracle He performs are manifestations of the Father's presence and activity through Him.

This assertion challenges any notion that Jesus acts independently of the Father. Instead, it reveals that Jesus' ministry is a perfect reflection of the Father's will. His teachings, miracles, and actions are direct revelations of God's character and purposes.

Evidence of the Works

Jesus urges His disciples to believe in His unity with the Father based on the evidence of His works: "Believe me when I say that I am in the Father and the Father is in me; or at least believe on the evidence of the works themselves." The miracles Jesus performed—healing the sick, raising the dead, feeding the multitudes, and calming the storm—are not just displays of power but signs that reveal His divine identity and the Father's presence in Him.

These works are consistent with the nature and mission of God as revealed in the Old Testament. They point to Jesus as the fulfillment of God's promises and the embodiment of His redemptive work. The miracles are tangible proof that Jesus is who He claims to be—the Son of God, one with the Father.

Theological Implications of Jesus' Unity with the Father

The Revelation of God

Jesus' unity with the Father is foundational to the Christian understanding of God. Through Jesus, we gain the fullest and most direct revelation of God's nature. Hebrews 1:1-3 states, "In the past God spoke to our ancestors through the prophets at many times and in various ways, but in these last days he has spoken to us by his Son, whom he appointed heir of all things, and through whom also he made the universe. The Son is the radiance of God's glory and the exact representation of his being, sustaining all things by his powerful word."

This revelation is not merely informational but relational. Jesus invites us to know God personally and intimately, experiencing His love, grace, and truth in our lives. Through Jesus, we are brought into a relationship with the Father, transforming our understanding of God from a distant deity to a loving Father.

The Assurance of Salvation

Jesus' unity with the Father provides the basis for the assurance of our salvation. As the one who perfectly reveals the Father and accomplishes His will, Jesus is uniquely qualified to be our Savior. His sacrificial death and resurrection are the ultimate expressions of the Father's love and justice, securing our redemption and reconciliation with God.

John 14:6 underscores this assurance: "Jesus answered, 'I am the way and the truth and the life. No one comes to the Father except through me.'" Jesus is the exclusive and sufficient means of salvation, providing a secure and unchanging foundation for our faith.

The Call to Reflect Jesus' Unity with the Father

Living in Union with Christ

Believers are called to live in union with Christ, reflecting His unity with the Father in our lives. This involves abiding in Jesus, allowing His words and Spirit to transform us and guide our actions. John 15:4-5 emphasizes this relationship: "Remain in me, as I also remain in you. No branch can bear fruit by itself; it must remain in the vine. Neither can you bear fruit unless you remain in me. I am the vine; you are the branches. If you remain in me and I in you, you will bear much fruit; apart from me you can do nothing."

Living in union with Christ means cultivating a deep and abiding relationship with Him, characterized by prayer, obedience, and dependence on His grace. As we remain in Him, His life flows through us, producing spiritual fruit and reflecting the Father's character to the world.

Witnessing to the World

Jesus' unity with the Father also compels us to witness to the world. Just as Jesus revealed the Father through His words and works, we are called to reveal Jesus through our lives. This involves sharing the Gospel, demonstrating God's love through acts of compassion and justice, and living in a way that reflects the values of God's kingdom.

Matthew 5:14-16 captures this calling: "You are the light of the world. A town built on a hill cannot be hidden.

Neither do people light a lamp and put it under a bowl. Instead they put it on its stand, and it gives light to everyone in the house. In the same way, let your light shine before others, that they may see your good deeds and glorify your Father in heaven."

Conclusion

John 14:9-11 reveals the profound truth of Jesus' divine nature and His unique unity with the Father. His declaration that anyone who has seen Him has seen the Father underscores His role as the ultimate revelation of God. Through His words and works, Jesus makes the Father's presence and character known, inviting us into a transformative relationship with God.

Understanding Jesus' unity with the Father deepens our faith and assures us of our salvation. It calls us to live in union with Christ, reflecting His character and mission in our lives. As we abide in Him and bear witness to His truth, we participate in the ongoing revelation of God's love and grace to the world.

This foundational truth shapes our identity as believers and empowers us to fulfill our calling as ambassadors of Christ. Through Jesus, we encounter the fullness of God's revelation, experiencing the profound reality of His oneness and the transformative power of His love.

CHAPTER 04

THE "I AM" STATEMENTS

The "I Am" statements of Jesus in the New Testament are profound declarations of His divinity and identity. These statements, particularly prominent in the Gospel of John, connect Jesus directly to the divine name revealed to Moses in the Old Testament. This chapter explores the significance of these statements, their Hebrew roots, and their theological implications.

The Divine Name: "I Am Who I Am"

Exodus 3:14 (NIV): "God said to Moses, 'I AM WHO I AM. This is what you are to say to the Israelites: 'I AM has sent me to you.'"

Hebrew Meaning and Analysis

The Hebrew phrase אֶהְיֶה אֲשֶׁר אֶהְיֶה (Ehyeh-Asher-Ehyeh) can be translated in various ways, including "I am who I am," "I will be what I will be," and "I am the Existing One." This self-revealed name of God emphasizes His eternal, self-existent, and unchanging nature.

- אֶהְיֶה (Ehyeh, Strong's H1961): The first person singular form of the verb "to be," indicating existence and presence.

- אֲשֶׁר (Asher, Strong's H834): A relative pronoun that can mean "who," "which," or "that."

- Theological Implications: This name reveals God's self-sufficiency, eternal existence, and unchanging nature. It signifies that God is not dependent on anything or anyone else for His existence.

Jesus and the "I Am" Statements

In the New Testament, Jesus uses the phrase "I Am" (Greek: ἐγώ εἰμι, ego eimi) multiple times, making direct connections to the divine name revealed in Exodus. These statements are particularly significant in the Gospel of John.

1. "I Am the Bread of Life" (John 6:35, 48, 51)

John 6:35 (NIV): "Then Jesus declared, 'I am the bread of life. Whoever comes to me will never go hungry, and whoever believes in me will never be thirsty.'"

- Context: Jesus makes this statement after feeding the 5,000, linking Himself to the provision of manna in the wilderness.

- Meaning: Jesus is the essential sustenance for spiritual life. Just as bread is necessary for physical survival, Jesus is necessary for spiritual sustenance and eternal life.

2. "I Am the Light of the World" (John 8:12)

John 8:12 (NIV): "When Jesus spoke again to the people, he said, 'I am the light of the world. Whoever follows me will never walk in darkness, but will have the light of life.'"

- Context: This statement is made during the Feast of Tabernacles, a festival with significant lighting ceremonies.

- Meaning: Jesus is the source of spiritual illumination and guidance. In a world darkened by sin, He brings the light of truth and life.

3. "I Am the Door of the Sheep" (John 10:7, 9)

John 10:7 (NIV): "Therefore Jesus said again, 'Very truly I tell you, I am the gate for the sheep.'"

- Context: Jesus contrasts Himself with false shepherds who exploit the sheep.

- Meaning: Jesus is the entry point to salvation. Through Him, believers gain access to God's kingdom and protection.

4. "I Am the Good Shepherd" (John 10:11, 14)

John 10:11 (NIV): "I am the good shepherd. The good shepherd lays down his life for the sheep."

- Context: This statement contrasts Jesus with hired hands who abandon the sheep.

- Meaning: Jesus is the caring and sacrificial leader of His followers. He knows His sheep and lays down His life for them.

5. "I Am the Resurrection and the Life" (John 11:25)

John 11:25 (NIV): "Jesus said to her, 'I am the resurrection and the life. The one who believes in me will live, even though they die.'"

- Context: Jesus makes this statement before raising Lazarus from the dead.

- Meaning: Jesus has power over life and death. He offers eternal life to all who believe in Him, conquering death through His resurrection.

6. "I Am the Way, the Truth, and the Life" (John 14:6)

John 14:6 (NIV): "Jesus answered, 'I am the way and the truth and the life. No one comes to the Father except through me.'"

- Context: Jesus speaks these words to His disciples during the Last Supper.

- Meaning: Jesus is the exclusive path to God, embodying truth and the source of all life.

7. "I Am the True Vine" (John 15:1, 5)

John 15:1 (NIV): "I am the true vine, and my Father is the gardener."

- Context: Jesus uses the imagery of a vine and branches to describe the relationship between Himself and His disciples.

- Meaning: Jesus is the source of spiritual vitality. Believers must remain connected to Him to bear fruit.

The Ultimate "I Am" Declaration: John 8:58

John 8:58 (NIV): "Very truly I tell you," Jesus answered, "before Abraham was born, I am!"

- Context: Jesus makes this declaration during a heated discussion with the Pharisees about His identity and authority.

- Meaning: By using the phrase "I Am," Jesus directly associates Himself with the divine name revealed to Moses. This statement asserts His pre-existence and divinity, affirming that He is eternal and uncreated.

Strong's Concordance Insights

- I Am (ἐγώ εἰμι, ego eimi, Strong's G1473 and G1510): This Greek phrase is used by Jesus to declare His identity and divinity, directly linking Himself to the divine name "I Am" in Exodus 3:14.

Theological Implications of the "I Am" Statements

1. Divine Identity: Jesus' "I Am" statements unequivocally affirm His divine nature. He is not just a prophet or teacher but God incarnate.

2. Revelation of God's Character: Each "I Am" statement reveals different facets of God's character – His provision, guidance, protection, truth, and life.

3. Mediator of God's Presence: Jesus as "I Am" bridges the gap between humanity and God. Through Him, we experience God's presence, truth, and life.

4. Source of Eternal Life: Jesus' identity as "I Am" underscores His role as the source of eternal life and salvation. Belief in Him is essential for reconciliation with God and eternal life.

Conclusion

The "I Am" statements of Jesus in the New Testament are profound declarations of His divinity and identity, connecting Him directly to the divine name revealed to Moses in Exodus. These statements reveal different aspects of Jesus' nature and mission, affirming His role as the eternal Son of God who offers salvation and eternal life. By understanding the Hebrew roots of "I Am" and the theological implications of Jesus' declarations, we gain a deeper appreciation of His divine authority and the profound mystery of His incarnation.

Jesus, the great "I Am," invites us to know Him, trust Him, and find life in Him.

The "I Am" Statements - The Bread of Life

The "I Am" statements of Jesus in the Gospel of John are profound declarations that reveal His divine nature and His unique role in God's redemptive plan. One of the most significant of these statements is found in John 6:35, where Jesus declares, "I am the bread of life." This statement not only emphasizes Jesus' divine identity but also illustrates His essential role in providing spiritual sustenance and eternal life. In this chapter, we will delve into the meaning and implications of Jesus' claim to be the bread of life, exploring how it reveals His divine nature and the spiritual nourishment He offers.

The Context of the Declaration

The Feeding of the Five Thousand

The declaration "I am the bread of life" occurs after the miraculous feeding of the five thousand, an event recorded in John 6:1-14. This miracle, where Jesus multiplies five loaves and two fish to feed a large crowd, serves as a backdrop to His teaching about the true bread from heaven. The crowd, amazed by the miracle, follows Jesus, seeking more signs and physical sustenance.

The Desire for Signs

In John 6:26-27, Jesus addresses the crowd's motivation: "Jesus answered, 'Very truly I tell you, you are looking for me, not because you saw the signs I performed but because you ate the loaves and had your fill. Do not work for food that spoils, but for food that endures to eternal life, which the Son of Man will give you. For on him God the Father has placed his seal of approval.'" Jesus redirects their focus from physical bread to the spiritual nourishment He offers.

Jesus as the Bread of Life

"I am the bread of life."

When Jesus declares, "I am the bread of life," He is making a profound statement about His divine identity and mission. This declaration is the first of the seven "I Am" statements in the Gospel of John, each of which reveals a different aspect of His divine nature and His relationship with humanity.

The metaphor of bread is rich with meaning. Bread was a staple food in the ancient Near East, essential for physical sustenance and survival. By identifying Himself as the bread of life, Jesus claims to be essential for spiritual sustenance and eternal life. Just as physical bread sustains the body, Jesus, the bread of life, sustains the soul.

The Divine Provision

The imagery of bread also connects to the Old Testament, specifically the manna provided by God to the Israelites in the wilderness. In John 6:31, the crowd references this provision: "Our ancestors ate the manna in the wilderness; as it is written: 'He gave them bread from heaven to eat.'" Jesus responds by distinguishing Himself from the manna: "Very truly I tell you, it is not Moses who has given you the bread from heaven, but it is my Father who gives you the true bread from heaven. For the bread of God is the bread that comes down from heaven and gives life to the world" (John 6:32-33).

By presenting Himself as the true bread from heaven, Jesus asserts that He is the ultimate fulfillment of God's provision, surpassing the temporary sustenance of manna. He is the divine provision for eternal life, sent by the Father to nourish and save humanity.

The Offer of Eternal Life

Spiritual Nourishment

In John 6:35, Jesus continues, "Whoever comes to me will never go hungry, and whoever believes in me will never be thirsty." This promise emphasizes the sufficiency and completeness of the spiritual nourishment He provides. To come to Jesus and believe in Him is to receive the sustenance that satisfies the deepest spiritual hunger and thirst.

This spiritual nourishment is not a one-time event but an ongoing relationship with Jesus. Believers are called to continually come to Him, drawing from His inexhaustible resources of grace, truth, and life. This ongoing relationship is central to the Christian faith, as it sustains and empowers believers to live according to God's will.

The Gift of Eternal Life

Jesus' declaration also underscores the gift of eternal life that He offers. In John 6:40, He states, "For my Father's will is that everyone who looks to the Son and believes in him shall have eternal life, and I will raise them up at the last day." Eternal life is not merely an extension of physical existence but a new quality of life characterized by an intimate relationship with God, beginning now and continuing forever.

This promise of eternal life is grounded in Jesus' divine authority and power. As the bread of life, He has the power to grant eternal life and to raise believers from the dead, ensuring that they share in His resurrection and glory.

The Rejection and Acceptance of the Bread of Life

The Crowd's Response

Despite the profound truths Jesus reveals, many in the crowd struggle to accept His claims. In John 6:41-42, we read, "At this the Jews there began to grumble about him because he said, 'I am the bread that came down from heaven.' They said, 'Is this not Jesus, the son of Joseph, whose father and mother we know? How can he now say, 'I came down from heaven'?'"

Their skepticism reflects a common challenge: recognizing the divine in the familiar. Jesus, whom they knew as the carpenter's son, is making claims that require them to see Him in a new light—as the divine Son of God, sent from heaven to provide eternal life.

The Call to Faith

Jesus responds by calling them to faith: "Stop grumbling among yourselves. No one can come to me unless the Father who sent me draws them, and I will raise them up at the last day. It is written in the Prophets: 'They will all be taught by God.' Everyone who has heard the Father and learned from him comes to me" (John 6:43-45).

Faith in Jesus as the bread of life is not merely intellectual assent but a transformative trust that leads to a relationship with Him. This faith is a response to God's drawing, as He reveals His Son to individuals and calls them to believe.

Theological Implications of Jesus as the Bread of Life
The Divine Nature of Jesus

Jesus' claim to be the bread of life underscores His divine nature. Only God can provide the spiritual nourishment and eternal life that Jesus offers. His ability to satisfy the deepest needs of the human soul and to grant eternal life is a testament to His divinity.

In John 6:51, Jesus further elaborates, "I am the living bread that came down from heaven. Whoever eats this bread will live forever. This bread is my flesh, which I will give for the life of the world." This statement foreshadows His sacrificial death on the cross, where He offers His body for the salvation of humanity. His willingness to give His life further demonstrates His divine love and commitment to God's redemptive plan.

The Invitation to a New Covenant

Jesus' declaration also invites believers into a new covenant relationship with God. This covenant is marked by the spiritual nourishment and eternal life that Jesus provides. In participating in this covenant, believers are called to remember and celebrate Jesus' sacrifice, as instituted in the Lord's Supper (communion). In this sacrament, the bread symbolizes His body given for us, and the wine His blood shed for the forgiveness of sins.

Conclusion

John 6:35 reveals the profound truth of Jesus' divine nature and His essential role as the bread of life. His declaration, "I am the bread of life," invites us to come to Him, believe in Him, and receive the spiritual nourishment and eternal life He offers. As the true bread from heaven, Jesus surpasses all other forms of sustenance, providing a relationship with God that satisfies our deepest needs and secures our eternal destiny.

Understanding Jesus as the bread of life deepens our faith and draws us into a transformative relationship with Him. It calls us to continually seek Him, trust in His provision, and live in the light of His grace and truth. As we partake of the bread of life, we experience the fullness of God's love and the abundant life He promises, both now and for eternity. This foundational truth shapes our identity as believers and empowers us to live out our faith, sharing the hope and nourishment we have received with a world in need.

The "I Am" - Before Abraham Was, I Am

In John 8:58, Jesus makes one of His most profound and controversial statements: "Very truly I tell you," Jesus answered, "Before Abraham was born, I am!" This declaration not only asserts His preexistence but also directly echoes God's self-identification in Exodus 3:14, where God reveals Himself to Moses as "I AM WHO I AM." In this chapter, we will delve into the significance of Jesus' statement, exploring how it reveals His divine nature and affirms His identity as God.

The Context of the Declaration

The Confrontation with the Jewish Leaders

The context of John 8:58 is a heated debate between Jesus and the Jewish leaders. Throughout John 8, Jesus engages in a dialogue that escalates in intensity, culminating in His bold declaration of preexistence and divinity. The Jewish leaders question His authority and legitimacy, accusing Him of blasphemy and even suggesting He has a demon.

The Question of Ancestry

The discussion centers around the issue of ancestry and spiritual heritage. The Jewish leaders pride themselves on being descendants of Abraham, claiming that their lineage guarantees their favor with God. Jesus challenges this assumption by pointing out that true children of Abraham would follow Abraham's example of faith and obedience to God. Instead, their rejection of Him reveals that they are not true children of Abraham.

Jesus' Declaration of Preexistence

"Before Abraham was born, I am!"

When Jesus declares, "Before Abraham was born, I am," He is making an extraordinary claim about His identity and existence. This statement has several profound implications:

1. Preexistence: Jesus asserts that He existed before Abraham, who lived approximately 2,000 years before Him. This claim transcends normal human existence and places Jesus in the realm of the eternal.

2. Divine Identity: By using the phrase "I am," Jesus directly identifies Himself with the divine name revealed to Moses in Exodus 3:14. In that passage, God says to Moses, "I AM WHO I AM. This is what you are to say to the Israelites: 'I AM has sent me to you.'" By echoing this divine self-identification, Jesus is claiming to be the eternal, self-existent God.

3. Authority and Supremacy: Jesus' use of "I am" underscores His authority and supremacy over all creation. He is not just a prophet or teacher but God incarnates, possessing all the attributes and authority of a deity.

The Reaction of the Jewish Leaders

Accusation of Blasphemy

The reaction of the Jewish leaders to Jesus' statement is immediate and hostile. In John 8:59, we read, "At this, they picked up stones to stone him, but Jesus hid himself, slipping away from the temple grounds." Their intention to stone Him reveals that they understood the gravity of His claim.

According to Jewish law, blasphemy—claiming to be God or equal with God—was punishable by death.

Their response underscores the radical nature of Jesus' declaration. It was not merely a philosophical or theological statement but a direct claim to divinity that challenged their understanding of God and their religious authority.

Theological Implications of Jesus' "I Am" Statement

The Eternal Nature of Jesus

Jesus' declaration of "I am" highlights His eternal nature. Unlike human beings who have a beginning and an end, Jesus exists outside of time. This eternal nature is a defining attribute of God. In Revelation 1:8, God declares, "I am the Alpha and the Omega, who is and who was and who is to come, the Almighty." By identifying Himself with the divine "I am," Jesus affirms His participation in this eternal nature.

This eternal nature is also reflected in the prologue of John's Gospel: "In the beginning was the Word, and the Word was with God, and the Word was God" (John 1:1). Jesus, as the Word, existed from the beginning with God, sharing in the divine essence and participating in creation.

The Self-Existence of Jesus

The phrase "I am" also emphasizes Jesus' self-existence. Unlike created beings who depend on God for their existence, Jesus is self-existent, deriving His being from Himself. This self-existence is a unique attribute of God, signifying His independence and sovereignty.

In Colossians 1:17, Paul writes, "He is before all things, and in him all things hold together." This statement affirms Jesus' role as the sustainer of all creation, highlighting His self-existence and divine authority.

The Revelation of God's Name

The Significance of "I AM"

The divine name "I AM WHO I AM" revealed to Moses in Exodus 3:14 is one of the most significant revelations of God's identity in the Old Testament. It signifies God's eternal, unchanging, and self-sufficient nature. By using the name "I am," Jesus is revealing that He shares in this divine identity and nature.

This revelation has profound implications for our understanding of God. It means that Jesus is not just a messenger of God but God Himself, come to dwell among us. In John 1:14, we read, "The Word became flesh and made his dwelling among us. We have seen his glory, the glory of the one and only Son, who came from the Father, full of grace and truth." Jesus, as the Word made flesh, reveals the fullness of God's glory and truth.

The Fulfillment of Old Testament Prophecies

Jesus' use of "I am" also fulfills Old Testament prophecies and expectations about the coming Messiah. Throughout the Old Testament, there are numerous references to the coming of a divine Savior who would redeem God's people. By identifying Himself with the divine name, Jesus fulfills these prophecies and reveals Himself as the long-awaited Messiah.

For example, in Isaiah 9:6, the prophet foretells the birth of a child who will be called "Wonderful Counselor, Mighty God, Everlasting Father, Prince of Peace." Jesus' declaration of "I am" confirms that He is this divine Savior, bringing salvation and peace to the world.

The Invitation to Believe

Faith in the Divine Jesus

Jesus' declaration of "I am" invites us to place our faith in Him as the eternal, self-existent God. This faith is not merely intellectual assent but a transformative trust that recognizes Jesus as the source of life, truth, and salvation. In John 8:24, Jesus warns, "If you do not believe that I am he, you will indeed die in your sins." Faith in Jesus as the "I am" is essential for receiving eternal life and experiencing the fullness of God's grace.

The Assurance of Salvation

Believing in Jesus as the "I am" provides the assurance of salvation and eternal life. In John 8:51, Jesus promises, "Very truly I tell you, whoever obeys my word will never see death." This promise is grounded in His divine authority and power. As the eternal God, Jesus has the power to grant eternal life and to save us from the consequences of sin.

The Call to Worship

Worshiping the Divine Jesus

Understanding Jesus as the "I am" calls us to worship Him as God. This worship involves recognizing His divinity, honoring His name, and submitting to His authority. In Revelation 5:12-13, we see a vision of worship in heaven, where the Lamb (Jesus) is praised alongside God the Father: "Worthy is the Lamb, who was slain, to receive power and wealth and wisdom and strength and honor and glory and praise!"

This worship is not confined to a particular place or time but is a way of life. It involves living in a manner that reflects the holiness, love, and truth of Jesus, and bearing witness to His divine identity in our words and actions.

Reflecting the Light of Jesus

As followers of Jesus, we are called to reflect His light and truth in the world. In John 8:12, Jesus declares, "I am the light of the world. Whoever follows me will never walk in darkness, but will have the light of life." By living in His light, we testify to His divinity and invite others to come to know Him as the eternal "I am."

Conclusion

John 8:58 reveals the profound truth of Jesus' divine nature through His declaration, "Before Abraham was born, I am!" This statement affirms His preexistence, self-existence, and eternal nature, identifying Him with the God who revealed Himself to Moses as "I AM WHO I AM." Understanding Jesus as the "I am" deepens our faith, assures us of our salvation, and calls us to worship and reflect His divine light in the world.

As we embrace Jesus as the eternal "I am," we are invited into a transformative relationship with Him, experiencing the fullness of His grace and truth. This foundational truth shapes our identity as believers and empowers us to live out our faith with confidence and joy, sharing the hope and light of the divine Jesus with a world in need.

The "I Am" - The Good Shepherd

In John 10:11, Jesus declares, "I am the good shepherd. The good shepherd lays down his life for the sheep." This statement is one of the seven "I Am" declarations in the Gospel of John, each revealing a different aspect of Jesus' divine nature and mission. By identifying Himself as the good shepherd, Jesus emphasizes His deep care, protection, and sacrificial love for His followers. In this chapter, we will explore the significance of Jesus' claim to be the good shepherd, delving into how it reveals His divine nature and His unique role in God's redemptive plan.

The Context of the Declaration

The Shepherd Imagery in Scripture

The imagery of a shepherd is deeply rooted in the biblical tradition, symbolizing care, guidance, and protection. In the Old Testament, God is often depicted as the shepherd of His people. For example, Psalm 23:1 famously begins, "The Lord is my shepherd; I shall not want." This metaphor portrays God as a loving and protective guide who leads His people to safety and provision.

The Contrast with False Shepherds

In John 10, Jesus contrasts Himself with false shepherds, who are more interested in their gain than the welfare of the sheep. These false shepherds, described as thieves and robbers, do not have the sheep's best interests at heart and abandon them in times of danger. By declaring Himself the good shepherd, Jesus distinguishes His true and selfless care for His followers.

Jesus as the Good Shepherd

"I am the good shepherd."

When Jesus declares, "I am the good shepherd," He is making a profound statement about His identity and mission. This declaration reveals several key aspects of His divine nature:

1. Care and Compassion: As the good shepherd, Jesus demonstrates a deep care and compassion for His sheep. He knows each one by name and leads them with gentleness and love. This personal relationship reflects the intimate knowledge and concern God has for each individual.

2. Protection and Guidance: The good shepherd protects the sheep from harm and guides them to safety. Jesus, as the good shepherd, provides spiritual protection from the dangers of sin and evil. He guides His followers on the path of righteousness, leading them to eternal life.

3. Sacrificial Love: The most significant aspect of Jesus' declaration is His willingness to lay down His life for the sheep. This sacrificial love is the ultimate expression of His divine nature and mission. Unlike hired hands who flee at the sight of danger, Jesus willingly sacrifices Himself to save His followers.

The Divine Nature of Jesus as the Good Shepherd

The Shepherd's Sacrifice

The declaration "The good shepherd lays down his life for the sheep" emphasizes the sacrificial nature of Jesus' love. This self-giving love is a defining characteristic of His divine nature. In John 10:17-18, Jesus further explains, "The reason my Father loves me is that I lay down my life—only to take it up again. No one takes it from me, but I lay it down of my own accord. I have authority to lay it down and authority to take it up again. This command I received from my Father."

Jesus' voluntary sacrifice is a powerful demonstration of His divine authority and love. His willingness to lay down His life underscores His commitment to God's redemptive plan and His profound love for humanity. This sacrificial act is the cornerstone of Christian faith, as it provides the means for salvation and reconciliation with God.

The Eternal Shepherd

Jesus' role as the good shepherd also highlights His eternal nature. Unlike human shepherds who are limited by time and mortality, Jesus' care for His sheep is everlasting. In Hebrews 13:20, Jesus is described as "that great Shepherd of the sheep," who, through the blood of the eternal covenant, brings believers into an everlasting relationship with God.

As the eternal shepherd, Jesus' guidance and protection extend beyond this life into eternity. His resurrection from the dead confirms His victory over sin and death, ensuring that His followers will share in His eternal life. This promise of eternal care and security is a profound assurance for believers.

The Relationship Between the Shepherd and the Sheep

Knowing the Sheep

In John 10:14, Jesus says, "I am the good shepherd; I know my sheep and my sheep know me." This mutual knowledge reflects a deep and personal relationship between Jesus and His followers. This relationship is characterized by trust, intimacy, and love.

The shepherd's knowledge of the sheep signifies Jesus' understanding of our individual needs, struggles, and desires. He is intimately aware of every aspect of our lives and cares for us with a tender and compassionate heart. This personal relationship is a source of comfort and strength, as it assures us that we are known and loved by our divine shepherd.

Following the Shepherd

The sheep's knowledge of the shepherd is equally important. Jesus' followers recognize His voice and respond to His guidance. In John 10:27, He states, "My sheep listen to my voice; I know them, and they follow me." This listening and following signify obedience and trust in Jesus' leadership.

Following the good shepherd involves a commitment to live according to His teachings and example. It means trusting Him to lead us in the right path, even when the way is difficult or uncertain. This obedience is not burdensome but is motivated by love and gratitude for the shepherd who laid down His life for us.

The Shepherd's Protection and Provision

Protection from Danger

As the good shepherd, Jesus provides protection from spiritual dangers. In John 10:28-29, He assures His followers, "I give them eternal life, and they shall never perish; no one will snatch them out of my hand. My Father, who has given them to me, is greater than all; no one can snatch them out of my Father's hand." This promise of protection underscores Jesus' divine power and authority to keep His followers safe from all harm.

This protection extends to the trials and challenges we face in life. Jesus, our good shepherd, is with us in every circumstance, guiding us through difficulties and shielding us from the attacks of the enemy. His presence provides security and peace, knowing that we are under His watchful care.

Provision for Needs

The good shepherd also provides for the needs of the sheep. In Psalm 23, the shepherd leads the sheep to green pastures and still waters, symbolizing God's provision for our physical, emotional, and spiritual needs. Jesus, as the good shepherd, ensures that His followers lack nothing necessary for their well-being.

In John 10:10, Jesus declares, "I have come that they may have life, and have it to the full." This abundant life encompasses all aspects of our existence, offering us a life rich in purpose, joy, and fulfillment. Jesus' provision is not limited to material needs but includes the spiritual nourishment that sustains our souls and leads us to eternal life.

The Invitation to Join the Flock

The Call to Follow Jesus

Jesus' declaration as the good shepherd is an invitation to join His flock. In John 10:16, He says, "I have other sheep that are not of this sheep pen. I must bring them also. They too will listen to my voice, and there shall be one flock and one shepherd." This invitation extends to all people, regardless of their background or past.

Following Jesus as the good shepherd involves responding to His call with faith and obedience. It means recognizing His voice and committing to walk in His ways. This decision leads to a transformative relationship with Jesus, where we experience His love, care, and guidance.

The Joy of Belonging

Joining the flock of the good shepherd brings the joy of belonging to a community of believers. As members of His flock, we are part of a larger family, united by our faith in Jesus and our shared experience of His love. This community provides support, encouragement, and accountability as we journey together in following the good shepherd.

Belonging to Jesus' flock also gives us a sense of purpose and mission. We are called to share the good news of the good shepherd with others, inviting them to experience the love and care that we have found in Him. This mission is a joyful privilege, as we participate in God's redemptive work in the world.

Conclusion

John 10:11 reveals the profound truth of Jesus' divine nature through His declaration, "I am the good shepherd." This statement emphasizes His care, protection, and sacrificial love for His followers, highlighting His unique role in God's redemptive plan. As the good shepherd, Jesus provides spiritual nourishment, eternal life, and the assurance of His constant presence and guidance.

Understanding Jesus as the good shepherd deepens our faith and draws us into a transformative relationship with Him. It calls us to follow Him with trust and obedience, knowing that He knows us intimately and cares for us deeply.

As we embrace Jesus as our good shepherd, we experience the fullness of His love and the abundant life He promises, both now and for eternity.

This foundational truth shapes our identity as believers and empowers us to live out our faith with confidence and joy, sharing the hope and care of the good shepherd with a world in need. Through Jesus, we encounter the divine shepherd who lays down His life for His sheep, leading us to green pastures and still waters, and guiding us on the path of righteousness for His name's sake.

The "I Am" - The Resurrection and the Life

In John 11:25, Jesus makes a profound declaration: "I am the resurrection and the life. The one who believes in me will live, even though they die." This statement is one of the seven "I Am" declarations in the Gospel of John, each revealing a different aspect of Jesus' divine nature and His mission. By identifying Himself as the resurrection and the life, Jesus emphasizes His power over life and death, and His ability to grant eternal life. In this chapter, we will explore the significance of Jesus' claim, delving into how it reveals His divine nature and the hope He offers to believers.

The Context of the Declaration

The Death of Lazarus

The context of Jesus' declaration is the death of His friend Lazarus. In John 11, we learn that Lazarus, the brother of Mary and Martha, is gravely ill. Despite receiving word of Lazarus' condition, Jesus delays His visit, and Lazarus dies. When Jesus finally arrives in Bethany, Lazarus has been in the tomb for four days, and his sisters are grieving their loss.

Martha's Grief and Faith

When Martha hears that Jesus has arrived, she goes out to meet Him and expresses her grief: "Lord, if you had been here, my brother would not have died" (John 11:21). Yet, even in her sorrow, Martha shows faith in Jesus' power, saying, "But I know that even now God will give you whatever you ask" (John 11:22). It is in this context of grief and faith that Jesus makes His profound declaration.

Jesus as the Resurrection and the Life

"I am the resurrection and the life."

Jesus' statement, "I am the resurrection and the life," is a direct assertion of His divine identity and authority over life and death. This declaration reveals several key aspects of His nature:

1. Source of Life: By identifying Himself as the resurrection and the life, Jesus asserts that He is the source of all life. He has the power to give life, sustain life, and restore

life. This claim goes beyond physical life to encompass spiritual and eternal life.

2. Power Over Death: Jesus' declaration emphasizes His authority over death. As the resurrection, He has the power to raise the dead and conquer death itself. This power is a defining attribute of His divinity.

3. Hope and Assurance: Jesus' words offer profound hope and assurance to believers. His promise that those who believe in Him will live, even though they die, provides a foundation for faith and a source of comfort in the face of death.

The Divine Nature of Jesus as the Resurrection and the Life

The Power to Give Life

In John 1:4, we read, "In him was life, and that life was the light of all mankind." This verse underscores that Jesus is the source of life, both physical and spiritual. His declaration as the resurrection and the life further affirms this truth. Jesus has the power to impart life to those who believe in Him, offering not just temporal life but eternal life.

This divine ability to give life is evident in His miracles, such as the raising of Jairus' daughter (Mark 5:21-43), the widow's son at Nain (Luke 7:11-17), and ultimately, Lazarus.

Each of these miracles points to Jesus' divine nature and His authority over life and death.

The Conquest of Death

Jesus' power over death is a central theme in the New Testament. In 1 Corinthians 15:54-55, Paul writes, "When the perishable has been clothed with the imperishable, and the mortal with immortality, then the saying that is written will come true: 'Death has been swallowed up in victory.' 'Where, O death, is your victory? Where, O death, is your sting?'" Jesus' resurrection is the ultimate victory over death, demonstrating His divine authority and the fulfillment of God's redemptive plan.

The resurrection of Lazarus serves as a powerful sign of Jesus' authority over death. When Jesus calls Lazarus out of the tomb, it is a clear demonstration of His divine power. This miracle not only validates Jesus' claim to be the resurrection and the life but also foreshadows His own resurrection, which is the cornerstone of Christian faith.

The Promise of Eternal Life

Belief and Eternal Life

In John 11:26, Jesus continues, "and whoever lives by believing in me will never die. Do you believe this?" This statement highlights the connection between belief in Jesus and the promise of eternal life. Faith in Jesus as the resurrection and the life is the key to experiencing the life He offers.

This promise is reiterated throughout the Gospel of John. In John 3:16, we read, "For God so loved the world that he gave his one and only Son, that whoever believes in him shall not perish but have eternal life." Jesus' mission is to offer eternal life to all who believe in Him, and this life is characterized by an unending relationship with God.

The Assurance of Resurrection

Jesus' promise of resurrection provides hope and assurance to believers facing the reality of death. In John 5:28-29, He states, "Do not be amazed at this, for a time is coming when all who are in their graves will hear his voice and come out—those who have done what is good will rise to live, and those who have done what is evil will rise to be condemned." This assurance of resurrection underscores the hope that Christians have in Christ, knowing that death is not the end but a transition to eternal life.

The Call to Believe

Martha's Confession of Faith

In response to Jesus' declaration, Martha makes a profound confession of faith: "Yes, Lord," she replied, "I believe that you are the Messiah, the Son of God, who is to come into the world" (John 11:27). Martha's faith serves as an example for all believers. Despite her grief and the apparent finality of death, she affirms her belief in Jesus' identity and His power to give life.

This confession of faith is a crucial aspect of the Christian response to Jesus' declaration. Believing in Jesus as the resurrection and the life involves trusting in His power, accepting His authority, and relying on His promise of eternal life.

An Invitation to All

Jesus' declaration as the resurrection and the life is an invitation to all people to believe in Him. It is a call to place faith in Him as the source of life and the conqueror of death. This invitation extends to everyone, regardless of their background or circumstances. Jesus' offer of life is universal and inclusive, inviting all to experience the hope and assurance He provides.

The Implications for Believers

Living in the Light of the Resurrection

Believing in Jesus as the resurrection and the life has profound implications for how we live. It calls us to live with hope, knowing that death has been conquered and that eternal life awaits us. This hope transforms our perspective on suffering, loss, and the challenges of life, enabling us to face them with faith and confidence in Jesus' promise.

Sharing the Hope of the Resurrection

As followers of Jesus, we are called to share the hope of the resurrection with others. This involves proclaiming the good news of Jesus' victory over death and inviting others to believe in Him. Our witness is a testament to the transformative power of Jesus' life and resurrection, offering hope to a world in need.

Conclusion

John 11:25 reveals the profound truth of Jesus' divine nature through His declaration, "I am the resurrection and the life." This statement emphasizes His power over life and death, and His ability to grant eternal life to all who believe in Him. As the resurrection and the life, Jesus offers hope and assurance, demonstrating His divine authority and fulfilling God's redemptive plan.

Understanding Jesus as the resurrection and the life deepens our faith and provides a foundation for our hope in eternal life. It calls us to believe in Him, live in the light of His resurrection, and share the hope He offers with others. Through Jesus, we encounter the divine source of life, who conquers death and brings us into an everlasting relationship with God. This foundational truth shapes our identity as believers and empowers us to live out our faith with confidence, joy, and the assurance of eternal life.

The "I Am" - The Way, the Truth, and the Life

In John 14:6, Jesus makes a profound and comprehensive declaration about His divine nature and unique role in God's redemptive plan: "I am the way, the truth, and the life. No one comes to the Father except through me." This statement encapsulates the essence of who Jesus is and the centrality of His role in salvation. By identifying Himself as the way, the truth, and the life, Jesus reveals His divine identity and the exclusive means by which humanity can be reconciled to God. In this chapter, we will delve into the significance of Jesus' claim, exploring how it reveals His divine nature and the path to eternal life.

The Context of the Declaration

The Upper Room Discourse

The setting of John 14 is the Upper Room, where Jesus is sharing a final meal with His disciples before His arrest and crucifixion. This section of John's Gospel, known as the Upper Room Discourse, contains some of Jesus' most intimate and profound teachings. It is in this context that Jesus seeks to comfort and prepare His disciples for the coming trials and His departure.

Thomas's Question

In John 14:5, Thomas expresses confusion and uncertainty about Jesus' statements regarding His departure and the way to where He is going: "Thomas said to him, 'Lord, we don't know where you are going, so how can we know the way?'" Jesus' response to Thomas's question is the profound declaration of His identity as the way, the truth, and the life.

Jesus as the Way

The Exclusive Path to the Father

When Jesus declares, "I am the way," He is asserting that He is the exclusive path to God the Father. This statement emphasizes the uniqueness of Jesus as the only means by which humanity can be reconciled to God. It underscores the necessity of faith in Jesus for salvation.

In the Old Testament, the concept of "the way" often referred to the path of righteousness and obedience to God's commands. By identifying Himself as the way, Jesus claims to be the fulfillment of this path. He is the living embodiment of God's righteousness and the only way to enter into a right relationship with God.

The Mediator Between God and Humanity

Jesus' role in the way highlights His function as the mediator between God and humanity. In 1 Timothy 2:5, Paul writes, "For there is one God and one mediator between God and mankind, the man Christ Jesus." As the mediator, Jesus bridges the gap caused by sin, providing access to the Father through His sacrificial death and resurrection.

This mediation is not just a matter of showing the way but of being the way. Jesus' life, death, and resurrection constitute the means by which believers are reconciled to God. His sacrifice on the cross atones for sin, and His resurrection conquers death, opening the way to eternal life.

Jesus as the Truth

The Embodiment of God's Truth

When Jesus declares, "I am the truth," He is claiming to be the ultimate revelation of God's truth. This statement emphasizes His divine nature as the source and embodiment of all truth. In John 1:14, we read, "The Word became flesh and made his dwelling among us. We have seen his glory, the glory of the one and only Son, who came from the Father, full of grace and truth."

Jesus' teachings, actions, and very presence reveal the truth of God's character and will. He is the living Word, the definitive revelation of who God is. In a world marred by deception and falsehood, Jesus stands as the absolute standard of truth, guiding believers into a deeper understanding of God and His purposes.

The Revelation of God's Will

As the truth, Jesus reveals God's will for humanity. His teachings provide insight into the nature of God's kingdom and the ethical demands of following Him. In John 8:31-32,

Jesus says, "If you hold to my teaching, you are really my disciples. Then you will know the truth, and the truth will set you free." This freedom is not merely intellectual but transformative, leading to a life aligned with God's will.

Jesus' role as the truth also involves exposing falsehood and confronting sin. His ministry often involved challenging the religious leaders of His time, who had distorted God's truth with their legalism and hypocrisy. By revealing the true nature of God and His will, Jesus calls His followers to live in integrity, honesty, and obedience to God's commands.

Jesus as the Life

The Source of Eternal Life

When Jesus declares, "I am the life," He asserts that He is the source of all life, both physical and spiritual. This statement emphasizes His divine power to grant eternal life to those who believe in Him. In John 1:4, we read, "In him was life, and that life was the light of all mankind."

Jesus' role as the life is most profoundly demonstrated in His resurrection. By rising from the dead, He conquers death and offers the promise of eternal life to all who trust in Him. This resurrection power is not limited to the future but is available to believers now, bringing new life and transformation.

The Fulfillment of Life's Purpose

As the life, Jesus offers a fullness and richness of life that transcends mere existence. In John 10:10, He declares, "I have come that they may have life, and have it to the full." This abundant life encompasses spiritual vitality, purpose, and joy, grounded in a relationship with Jesus.

Jesus' promise of life extends beyond the temporal to the eternal. Believers are assured of eternal life with God, a life characterized by perfect fellowship, love, and worship. This promise provides hope and motivation for living faithfully in the present, knowing that our ultimate destiny is secure in Christ.

The Exclusivity of Jesus' Claim

No One Comes to the Father Except Through Me

Jesus' declaration, "No one comes to the Father except through me," underscores the exclusivity of His role in salvation. This statement challenges the notion that there are multiple paths to God, affirming that Jesus is the only way to a relationship with the Father.

This exclusivity is not a matter of exclusion but of invitation. Jesus invites all people to come to the Father through Him, offering the way, the truth, and the life to everyone who believes. This invitation is inclusive and universal, extending to all who will place their faith in Jesus.

The Necessity of Faith in Jesus

The exclusivity of Jesus' claim emphasizes the necessity of faith in Him for salvation. In John 3:16, we read, "For God so loved the world that he gave his one and only Son, that whoever believes in him shall not perish but have eternal life." Faith in Jesus is the means by which we receive the life He offers and enter into a relationship with the Father.

This faith involves more than intellectual assent; it requires trust, commitment, and obedience. Believing in Jesus as the way, the truth, and the life means entrusting our lives to Him, following His teachings, and relying on His promises.

The Implications for Believers

Living in the Way

Believing in Jesus as the way calls us to follow Him with trust and obedience. This involves aligning our lives with His teachings, seeking to live in accordance with His will, and relying on His guidance. Following Jesus as the way leads to a life of righteousness, purpose, and fulfillment, grounded in a relationship with Him.

Abiding in the Truth

As followers of Jesus, we are called to abide in His truth. This means holding fast to His teachings, rejecting falsehood, and living with integrity and honesty. Abiding in the truth transforms our minds and hearts, leading us to a deeper understanding of God and His purposes.

Experiencing the Life

Believing in Jesus as the life invites us to experience the fullness of life He offers. This involves embracing the abundant life He promises, characterized by spiritual vitality, joy, and purpose. It also means living with the assurance of eternal life, knowing that our ultimate destiny is secure in Christ.

Conclusion

John 14:6 reveals the profound truth of Jesus' divine nature through His declaration, "I am the way, the truth, and the life. No one comes to the Father except through me." This statement emphasizes Jesus' unique and exclusive role in salvation, highlighting His identity as the path to God, the embodiment of truth, and the source of life.

Understanding Jesus as the way, the truth, and the life deepens our faith and provides a foundation for our relationship with God. It calls us to follow Him with trust and obedience, abide in His truth, and experience the fullness of life He offers. As we embrace Jesus' declaration, we are invited into a transformative relationship with Him, experiencing the hope, assurance, and joy that come from knowing the way, the truth, and the life.

This foundational truth shapes our identity as believers and empowers us to live out our faith with confidence and joy, sharing the hope and life we have found in Jesus with a world in need. Through Jesus, we encounter the divine source of salvation, truth, and life, leading us into a deeper relationship with God and a life of purpose and fulfillment.

The "I Am" - The Way, the Truth, and the Life

In John 14:6, Jesus makes a profound and all-encompassing declaration: "I am the way, the truth, and the life. No one comes to the Father except through me." This statement is not only a powerful affirmation of His divine identity but also a comprehensive summary of His mission and the unique role He plays in God's plan for humanity. By identifying Himself as the way, the truth, and the life, Jesus reveals the depth of His divine nature and His essential place in the salvation of mankind. This chapter explores the significance of this declaration, delving into its theological implications and what it reveals about the nature of Jesus Christ.

The Context of the Declaration

The Upper Room Discourse

The setting for Jesus' declaration is the Upper Room Discourse, a series of teachings and conversations Jesus had with His disciples on the night before His crucifixion. This discourse, found in John 13-17, is filled with intimate and profound teachings as Jesus prepares His disciples for His imminent departure. The context of John 14:6 is Jesus comforting His disciples, who are troubled by His announcement that He will soon leave them.

Thomas's Question

In John 14:5, Thomas, one of Jesus' disciples, expresses confusion about Jesus' statement that He is going to prepare a place for them: "Lord, we don't know where you are going, so how can we know the way?" Jesus' response to Thomas is the profound declaration that He is the way, the truth, and the life. This answer is meant to reassure and guide His disciples, emphasizing that through Him, they have access to the Father.

Jesus as the Way

The Exclusive Path to the Father

When Jesus declares, "I am the way," He is asserting that He is the only means by which humanity can come into a right relationship with God the Father. This statement highlights the exclusivity of Jesus as the mediator between God and man. In a world where many paths to spirituality and God are proposed, Jesus unequivocally states that He alone is the path to the Father.

This exclusivity is emphasized in Jesus' teaching throughout the New Testament. In Acts 4:12, Peter echoes this truth, saying, "Salvation is found in no one else, for there is no other name under heaven given to mankind by which we must be saved." Jesus' role as the way underscores His divine authority and the necessity of faith in Him for salvation.

The Mediator and High Priest

Jesus' role as the way also signifies His function as the mediator and high priest. As the mediator, Jesus bridges the gap between a holy God and sinful humanity. His sacrificial death on the cross provides the means for reconciliation and peace with God. In Hebrews 10:19-20, we read, "Therefore, brothers and sisters, since we have confidence to enter the Most Holy Place by the blood of Jesus, by a new and living way opened for us through the curtain, that is, his body."

As our high priest, Jesus intercedes on our behalf, continually presenting us before the Father. His priestly ministry ensures that we have ongoing access to God and can approach Him with confidence and boldness.

Jesus as the Truth

The Embodiment of Divine Truth

When Jesus declares, "I am the truth," He is claiming to be the ultimate revelation of God's truth. This statement affirms that all truth is found in Him and that He perfectly embodies the nature and character of God. In John 1:14, we read, "The Word became flesh and made his dwelling among us. We have seen his glory, the glory of the one and only Son, who came from the Father, full of grace and truth."

Jesus is the living Word, the ultimate expression of God's truth and reality. His teachings, actions, and very presence reveal the nature of God and His will for humanity. As the truth, Jesus is the standard by which all other claims of truth are measured.

The Revelation of God's Character

Jesus' role as the truth also involves revealing the character of God. Throughout His ministry, Jesus demonstrated God's love, compassion, holiness, and righteousness. In John 14:9, Jesus tells Philip, "Anyone who has seen me has seen the Father." This statement underscores that in seeing and knowing Jesus, we see and know God the Father.

Jesus' life and teachings reveal God's desire for a relationship with humanity and His plan for redemption. His truth confronts sin and falsehood, calling people to repentance and a new way of living in alignment with God's will.

Jesus as the Life

The Source of Eternal Life

When Jesus declares, "I am the life," He is affirming that He is the source of all life, both physical and spiritual. This statement emphasizes His divine power to grant life and His role in sustaining it. In John 1:4, we read, "In him was life, and that life was the light of all mankind." Jesus, as the life, is the source of all that is living and vibrant.

This divine attribute is most profoundly demonstrated in Jesus' resurrection. By rising from the dead, Jesus conquers death and offers eternal life to all who believe in Him. His resurrection is the cornerstone of Christian faith, providing hope and assurance of eternal life for believers.

The Fullness of Life

Jesus' promise of life extends beyond mere existence to a fullness and richness of life that is characterized by spiritual vitality, purpose, and joy. In John 10:10, Jesus says, "I have come that they may have life, and have it to the full." This abundant life is a life lived in relationship with God, experiencing His love, grace, and guidance.

The life that Jesus offers transforms every aspect of our existence, giving us a sense of purpose and direction. It is a life that is marked by the indwelling presence of the Holy Spirit, who empowers and sustains us in our walk with God.

The Exclusivity of Jesus' Claim

No One Comes to the Father Except Through Me

Jesus' declaration, "No one comes to the Father except through me," underscores the exclusivity of His role in salvation. This statement challenges the notion that there are multiple paths to God, affirming that Jesus is the only way to a relationship with the Father.

This exclusivity is not about exclusion but about the unique and singular nature of Jesus' person and work. As the incarnate Word of God, Jesus alone possesses the authority and power to bring us into communion with God. His life, death, and resurrection are the means by which we are reconciled to the Father.

The Necessity of Faith in Jesus

The exclusivity of Jesus' claim emphasizes the necessity of faith in Him for salvation. In John 3:16, we read, "For God so loved the world that he gave his one and only Son, that whoever believes in him shall not perish but have eternal life." Faith in Jesus is the means by which we receive the life He offers and enter into a relationship with the Father.

This faith is not merely intellectual assent but involves trust, commitment, and obedience. Believing in Jesus as the way, the truth, and the life means entrusting our lives to Him, following His teachings, and relying on His promises.

The Implications for Believers

Living in the Way

Believing in Jesus as the way calls us to follow Him with trust and obedience. This involves aligning our lives with His teachings, seeking to live in accordance with His will, and relying on His guidance. Following Jesus as the way leads to a life of righteousness, purpose, and fulfillment, grounded in a relationship with Him.

Abiding in the Truth

As followers of Jesus, we are called to abide in His truth. This means holding fast to His teachings, rejecting falsehood, and living with integrity and honesty. Abiding in the truth transforms our minds and hearts, leading us to a deeper understanding of God and His purposes.

Experiencing the Life

Believing in Jesus as the life invites us to experience the fullness of life He offers. This involves embracing the abundant life He promises, characterized by spiritual vitality, joy, and purpose. It also means living with the assurance of eternal life, knowing that our ultimate destiny is secure in Christ.

Conclusion

John 14:6 reveals the profound truth of Jesus' divine nature through His declaration, "I am the way, the truth, and the life. No one comes to the Father except through me." This statement emphasizes Jesus' unique and exclusive role in salvation, highlighting His identity as the path to God, the embodiment of truth, and the source of life.

Understanding Jesus as the way, the truth, and the life deepens our faith and provides a foundation for our relationship with God. It calls us to follow Him with trust and obedience, abide in His truth, and experience the fullness of life He offers. As we embrace Jesus' declaration, we are invited into a transformative relationship with Him, experiencing the hope, assurance, and joy that come from knowing the way, the truth, and the life.

This foundational truth shapes our identity as believers and empowers us to live out our faith with confidence and joy, sharing the hope and life we have found in Jesus with a world in need. Through Jesus, we encounter the divine source of salvation, truth, and life, leading us into a deeper relationship with God and a life of purpose and fulfillment.

The "I Am" - The True Vine

In John 15:1, Jesus declares, "I am the true vine, and my Father is the gardener." This statement, one of the seven "I Am" declarations in the Gospel of John, reveals profound truths about Jesus' divine nature and the essential relationship between Him and His followers. By identifying Himself as the true vine, Jesus emphasizes His role as the source of spiritual life and growth. This chapter will delve into the significance of Jesus' claim, exploring how it reveals His divine nature and the vital connection between believers and Christ.

The Context of the Declaration

The Upper Room Discourse

The setting for Jesus' declaration is the Upper Room, where Jesus is sharing His final moments with His disciples before His crucifixion. This section of John's Gospel, known as the Upper Room Discourse (John 13-17), contains some of Jesus' most intimate and profound teachings. It is within this context of preparing His disciples for His departure and their future ministry that Jesus presents the metaphor of the vine and the branches.

Jesus as the True Vine

"I am the true vine."

When Jesus declares, "I am the true vine," He is using a powerful metaphor to describe His relationship with His followers. The imagery of the vine is deeply rooted in Jewish tradition and Scripture. In the Old Testament, Israel is often depicted as a vine or vineyard planted by God. For example, Psalm 80:8-9 says, "You transplanted a vine from Egypt; you drove out the nations and planted it. You cleared the ground for it, and it took root and filled the land."

By calling Himself the true vine, Jesus is making a significant claim about His identity and mission. He is positioning Himself as the fulfillment of what Israel was meant to be—a source of life and blessing to the world. Unlike the vine of Israel, which often failed to produce good fruit, Jesus, as the true vine, perfectly fulfills God's purpose and provides the means for believers to bear spiritual fruit.

The Divine Nature of Jesus as the True Vine

The Source of Spiritual Life

Jesus' declaration as the true vine emphasizes His role as the source of spiritual life. Just as a vine provides the necessary nutrients and support for its branches to grow and bear fruit, Jesus provides the spiritual sustenance and strength that believers need to thrive. In John 15:4-5, Jesus explains, "Remain in me, as I also remain in you. No branch can bear fruit by itself; it must remain in the vine. Neither can you bear fruit unless you remain in me. I am the vine; you are the branches. If you remain in me and I in you, you will bear much fruit; apart from me you can do nothing."

This connection between the vine and the branches highlights the intimate and life-giving relationship between Jesus and His followers. As the true vine, Jesus is the source of all spiritual vitality, enabling believers to grow in faith, produce good works, and live according to God's will.

The Gardener's Role

In the same verse, Jesus also identifies God the Father as the gardener: "and my Father is the gardener." The gardener's role is to tend the vine, ensuring its health and productivity. This involves pruning branches that bear fruit to make them even more fruitful and removing those that do not bear fruit. John 15:2 states, "He cuts off every branch in me that bears no fruit, while every branch that does bear fruit he prunes so that it will be even more fruitful."

This imagery underscores the divine nature of Jesus and the Father's active involvement in the lives of believers. The Father's pruning is an essential aspect of spiritual growth, as it removes anything that hinders fruitfulness and promotes greater spiritual maturity.

The Vital Connection Between Believers and Christ

Abiding in the Vine

One of the central themes of Jesus' metaphor is the importance of abiding in the vine. To abide means to remain or stay connected. In John 15:4, Jesus says, "Remain in me, as I also remain in you." This mutual abiding is the key to spiritual vitality and fruitfulness. As believers remain in Christ, they draw from His life-giving presence and power, which enables them to grow and produce fruit.

Abiding in Christ involves maintaining a close and continuous relationship with Him. This includes regular prayer, reading and meditating on His Word, and living in obedience to His commands. As believers abide in Christ, they experience His presence, guidance, and strength in their daily lives.

The Result of Abiding: Bearing Fruit

The primary result of abiding in Christ is bearing fruit. In John 15:5, Jesus promises, "If you remain in me and I in you, you will bear much fruit; apart from me you can do nothing." Bearing fruit is a natural outcome of a healthy connection to the vine. This fruit includes the development of Christ-like character, such as the fruit of the Spirit described in Galatians 5:22-23—love, joy, peace, patience, kindness, goodness, faithfulness, gentleness, and self-control.

Bearing fruit also involves participating in God's work in the world. This includes sharing the Gospel, serving others, and living out the principles of God's kingdom. As believers bear fruit, they glorify God and demonstrate the reality of His presence in their lives.

The Implications for Believers

Dependence on Christ

Jesus' declaration as the true vine emphasizes the necessity of dependence on Him for spiritual life and growth.

Believers cannot produce spiritual fruit on their own; they must remain connected to Christ, drawing from His strength and sustenance. This dependence requires humility, recognizing that apart from Him, we can do nothing.

The Assurance of God's Care

The imagery of the vine and the gardener provides assurance of God's care and involvement in our lives. The Father's pruning, though sometimes painful, is a sign of His love and commitment to our growth. It is through this pruning that we become more fruitful and effective in our walk with Christ.

The Call to Abide

Believers are called to abide in Christ, maintaining a close and continuous relationship with Him. This abiding involves intentional practices such as prayer, reading Scripture, worship, and obedience. As we abide in Christ, we experience His presence and power in our lives, leading to spiritual growth and fruitfulness.

The Ultimate Purpose: Glorifying God

In John 15:8, Jesus states, "This is to my Father's glory, that you bear much fruit, showing yourselves to be my disciples." The ultimate purpose of abiding in Christ and bearing fruit is to glorify God. As believers live fruitful lives, they reflect the character and love of Christ, bringing honor to the Father and demonstrating the reality of their discipleship.

Conclusion

John 15:1 reveals the profound truth of Jesus' divine nature through His declaration, "I am the true vine." This statement emphasizes His role as the source of spiritual life and growth, highlighting the vital connection between believers and Christ. As the true vine, Jesus provides the sustenance and strength necessary for believers to thrive and bear fruit.

Understanding Jesus as the true vine deepens our faith and underscores the importance of abiding in Him. It calls us to maintain a close and continuous relationship with Christ, drawing from His life-giving presence and power. As we abide in Him, we experience His guidance and strength, leading to spiritual vitality and fruitfulness.

This foundational truth shapes our identity as believers and empowers us to live out our faith with confidence and joy, sharing the hope and life we have found in Jesus with a world in need. Through Jesus, we encounter the divine source of spiritual growth and fruitfulness, leading us into a deeper relationship with God and a life of purpose and fulfillment.

The Significance of God's Name "I Am" Revealed to Moses in Exodus 3:14 and Its Connection to Jesus

The revelation of God's name "I Am" to Moses in Exodus 3:14 is one of the most profound moments in the Old Testament. This declaration not only reveals God's eternal and self-existent nature but also lays the groundwork for understanding the identity and mission of Jesus Christ in the New Testament. This chapter explores the significance of God's name "I Am," its meaning in the Hebrew context, and its direct connection to Jesus as revealed in the New Testament.

God's Name "I Am" in Exodus 3:14

Exodus 3:14 (NIV): "God said to Moses, 'I AM WHO I AM. This is what you are to say to the Israelites: 'I AM has sent me to you.'"

Context and Analysis

The revelation of God's name occurs during Moses' encounter with the burning bush. God calls Moses to deliver the Israelites from slavery in Egypt, and Moses asks God for His name to validate his mission.

1. The Burning Bush: The bush that burns without being consumed symbolizes God's holy and eternal presence.

2. Moses' Question: Moses asks God what name he should give to the Israelites to authenticate his mission.

3. God's Response: God reveals His name as "I AM WHO I AM" (Hebrew: אֶהְיֶה אֲשֶׁר אֶהְיֶה, Ehyeh-Asher-Ehyeh).

Hebrew Meaning and Theological Implications

- אֶהְיֶה (Ehyeh, Strong's H1961): The first person singular form of the verb "to be," indicating existence and presence.

- אֲשֶׁר (Asher, Strong's H834): A relative pronoun that can mean "who," "which," or "that."

The phrase אֶהְיֶה אֲשֶׁר אֶהְיֶה can be translated in various ways:

- "I am who I am"

- "I will be what I will be"

- "I am what I am"

- "I will become what I choose to become"

- "I am the Existing One"

This name reveals several key attributes of God:

1. Self-Existence: God is self-existent and independent, not contingent upon anything or anyone else.

2. Eternality: God exists outside of time and space, eternal and unchanging.

3. Sovereignty: God has the power to be whatever He chooses to be, indicating His sovereign control over all creation.

Connection to Jesus in the New Testament

The "I Am" statements of Jesus in the New Testament directly connect Him to the divine name revealed to Moses, affirming His divinity and eternal nature. These statements are particularly prominent in the Gospel of John.

1. "I Am the Bread of Life" (John 6:35, 48, 51)

John 6:35 (NIV): "Then Jesus declared, 'I am the bread of life. Whoever comes to me will never go hungry, and whoever believes in me will never be thirsty.'"

- Significance: Jesus presents Himself as the essential sustenance for spiritual life, just as God provided manna in the wilderness.

2. "I Am the Light of the World" (John 8:12)

John 8:12 (NIV): "When Jesus spoke again to the people, he said, 'I am the light of the world. Whoever follows me will never walk in darkness, but will have the light of life.'"

- Significance: Jesus declares Himself the source of spiritual illumination and guidance, echoing God's presence as the pillar of fire leading Israel through the desert.

3. "I Am the Door of the Sheep" (John 10:7, 9)

John 10:7 (NIV): "Therefore Jesus said again, 'Very truly I tell you, I am the gate for the sheep.'"

- Significance: Jesus is the entry point to salvation, emphasizing His role as the mediator between God and humanity.

4. "I Am the Good Shepherd" (John 10:11, 14)

John 10:11 (NIV): "I am the good shepherd. The good shepherd lays down his life for the sheep."

- Significance: Jesus is the caring and sacrificial leader who knows His followers intimately and gives His life for them, fulfilling the shepherd imagery of the Old Testament.

5. "I Am the Resurrection and the Life" (John 11:25)

John 11:25 (NIV): "Jesus said to her, 'I am the resurrection and the life. The one who believes in me will live, even though they die.'"

- Significance: Jesus asserts His power over life and death, offering eternal life to all who believe in Him.

6. "I Am the Way, the Truth, and the Life" (John 14:6)

John 14:6 (NIV): "Jesus answered, 'I am the way and the truth and the life. No one comes to the Father except through me.'"

- Significance: Jesus declares Himself the exclusive path to God, embodying the ultimate truth and source of life.

7. "I Am the True Vine" (John 15:1, 5)

John 15:1 (NIV): "I am the true vine, and my Father is the gardener."

- Significance: Jesus is the source of spiritual vitality and growth, emphasizing the importance of remaining connected to Him.

The Ultimate "I Am" Declaration: John 8:58

John 8:58 (NIV): "Very truly I tell you," Jesus answered, "before Abraham was born, I am!"

- Context: Jesus makes this declaration during a heated discussion with the Pharisees about His identity and authority.

- Meaning: By using the phrase "I Am," Jesus directly associates Himself with the divine name revealed to Moses. This statement asserts His pre-existence and divinity, affirming that He is eternal and uncreated.

Strong's Concordance Insights

- I Am (ἐγώ εἰμι, ego eimi, Strong's G1473 and G1510): This Greek phrase is used by Jesus to declare His identity and divinity, directly linking Himself to the divine name "I Am" in Exodus 3:14.

Theological Implications

1. Affirmation of Divinity: Jesus' use of "I Am" unequivocally affirms His divine nature, identifying Himself with the God of the Old Testament.

2. Eternal Existence: Jesus' declarations highlight His eternal existence, pre-dating Abraham and existing before the creation of the world.

3. Revelation of God's Character: Each "I Am" statement reveals different facets of God's character – His provision, guidance, protection, truth, and life – all embodied in Jesus.

4. Mediator of God's Presence: Jesus, as "I Am," bridges the gap between humanity and God. Through Him, believers experience God's presence, truth, and life.

5. Source of Eternal Life: Jesus' identity as "I Am" underscores His role as the source of eternal life and salvation. Belief in Him is essential for reconciliation with God and eternal life.

Conclusion

The significance of God's name "I Am" revealed to Moses in Exodus 3:14 is profound, revealing God's self-existence, eternality, and sovereignty. Jesus' use of "I Am" in the New Testament directly connects Him to this divine name, affirming His divinity and eternal nature. These statements provide a deep insight into the identity and mission of Jesus, emphasizing His role as the mediator between God and humanity and the source of eternal life. By understanding the connection between the divine name in the

Old Testament and Jesus' declarations in the New Testament, we gain a richer understanding of the continuity and coherence of God's redemptive plan and the centrality of Jesus in it.

CHAPTER 05

JESUS' PRE-EXISTENCE AND GLORY

In John 17:5, Jesus prays, "And now, Father, glorify me in your own presence with the glory that I had with you before the world existed." This profound statement is part of Jesus' High Priestly Prayer, a deeply significant prayer offered on the night before His crucifixion. This verse reveals critical aspects of Jesus' divine nature, including His pre-existence and the glory He shared with the Father before the creation of the world. In this chapter, we will delve into the significance of Jesus' prayer, exploring how it reveals His divine nature and eternal glory.

The Context of the Prayer

The High Priestly Prayer

John 17 records what is often referred to as Jesus' High Priestly Prayer. In this prayer, Jesus intercedes for Himself, His disciples, and all future believers. This prayer occurs just before His arrest and crucifixion, marking a pivotal moment in His earthly ministry. It reveals Jesus' heart and mission, His relationship with the Father, and His deep concern for His followers.

Jesus' Pre-Existence

"The glory that I had with you before the world existed."

Jesus' prayer in John 17:5 directly references His pre-existence, affirming that He existed with the Father before the creation of the world. This statement is a clear assertion of Jesus' divine nature. Unlike created beings, Jesus has no beginning; He exists eternally with the Father.

In John 1:1-2, we read, "In the beginning was the Word, and the Word was with God, and the Word was God. He was with God in the beginning." These verses emphasize that Jesus, the Word, was present with God from the very beginning, participating in creation and sharing in the divine nature. This pre-existence sets Jesus apart from all other beings, affirming His deity and eternal existence.

The Glory of Jesus

The Glory Shared with the Father

When Jesus speaks of "the glory that I had with you before the world existed," He is referring to the divine glory He shared with the Father in eternity. This glory is an essential aspect of His divine nature. In the Old Testament, the glory of God is often associated with His presence, power, and majesty. For example, in Exodus 33:18-23, Moses asks to see God's glory, and God reveals His goodness and sovereignty.

Jesus' reference to His pre-existent glory underscores His equality with the Father. He is not a lesser being but shares fully in the divine essence and attributes. This shared glory is a testament to His divine identity and His intimate relationship with the Father.

The Manifestation of Glory in the Incarnation

Although Jesus temporarily set aside His divine glory to become human, His life and ministry revealed glimpses of this glory. In John 1:14, we read, "The Word became flesh and made his dwelling among us. We have seen his glory, the glory of the one and only Son, who came from the Father, full of grace and truth." Jesus' miracles, teachings, and very presence revealed the glory of God in human form.

The Transfiguration is a significant event where Jesus' divine glory is momentarily unveiled. In Matthew 17:1-2, we read, "After six days Jesus took with him Peter, James and John the brother of James, and led them up a high mountain by themselves. There he was transfigured before them. His face shone like the sun, and his clothes became as white as the light." This event provided the disciples with a glimpse of Jesus' true, divine nature and the glory He shared with the Father.

The Restoration of Glory

The Request for Glorification

In John 17:5, Jesus prays for the restoration of His pre-existent glory. This request is not just for His own benefit but for the fulfillment of God's redemptive plan. The glorification of Jesus is closely linked to His crucifixion, resurrection, and ascension. Through these events, Jesus' divine nature and mission are fully revealed and affirmed.

The glorification of Jesus involves His return to the Father's presence, where He once again fully shares in the divine glory. This return to glory is also an affirmation of His victory over sin and death, confirming His role as the Savior and Redeemer of humanity.

The Implications for Believers

Jesus' prayer for glorification has profound implications for believers. In John 17:24, He prays, "Father, I want those you have given me to be with me where I am, and to see my glory, the glory you have given me because you loved me before the creation of the world." Jesus' desire is for

His followers to share in His glory and to be with Him eternally.

This promise of sharing in Jesus' glory provides hope and assurance for believers. It reminds us that our ultimate destiny is to be with Christ, experiencing the fullness of His presence and glory. This hope encourages us to live faithfully and expectantly, knowing that we are destined for a glorious future with our Lord.

Theological Implications of Jesus' Pre-Existence and Glory

Affirmation of Jesus' Divinity

Jesus' reference to His pre-existent glory is a clear affirmation of His divinity. It establishes that Jesus is not merely a prophet or a great teacher but God Himself, who existed with the Father from eternity. This truth is central to Christian theology, underscoring the uniqueness and supremacy of Jesus Christ.

The affirmation of Jesus' divinity also underscores the significance of the Incarnation. The fact that the eternal, glorious Son of God took on human flesh to redeem humanity is a profound mystery and a demonstration of God's incredible love and grace.

The Unity of the Trinity

Jesus' prayer also highlights the unity of the Trinity. The shared glory between the Father and the Son points to their essential unity and mutual indwelling. While the distinct persons of the Trinity have different roles in the economy of salvation, they are one in essence and purpose.

This unity is a model for the church. In His prayer, Jesus also prays for the unity of His followers, reflecting the unity He shares with the Father (John 17:21-23). Believers are called to live in unity, reflecting the love and harmony of the Triune God.

The Call to Reflect Jesus' Glory

Living as Reflectors of His Glory

As followers of Christ, we are called to reflect His glory in our lives. This involves living in a way that honors Him and demonstrates His presence in us. In 2 Corinthians 3:18, Paul writes, "And we all, who with unveiled faces contemplate the Lord's glory, are being transformed into his image with ever-increasing glory, which comes from the Lord, who is the Spirit."

This transformation is a process of sanctification, where we grow in Christ likeness and reflect more of His character and glory. It involves surrendering to the Holy Spirit's work in our lives and allowing Him to shape us into the image of Christ.

Bearing Witness to His Glory

We are also called to bear witness to Jesus' glory in the world. This involves sharing the Gospel, living out our faith with integrity, and demonstrating the love and grace of Christ to others. Our lives should point to the reality of Jesus' divine nature and the hope we have in Him.

In Matthew 5:16, Jesus exhorts His followers, "Let your light shine before others, that they may see your good deeds and glorify your Father in heaven." By reflecting Jesus' glory in our actions and attitudes, we draw others to Him and bring glory to God.

Conclusion

John 17:5 reveals the profound truth of Jesus' divine nature through His prayer, "And now, Father, glorify me in your own presence with the glory that I had with you before the world existed." This statement emphasizes Jesus' pre-existence and the eternal glory He shares with the Father. It underscores His divinity and the intimate relationship within the Trinity.

Understanding Jesus' pre-existence and glory deepens our faith and provides a foundation for our hope in eternal life. It calls us to reflect His glory in our lives, living in a way that honors Him and bears witness to His divine nature. As we embrace the truth of Jesus' pre-existence and glory, we are invited into a transformative relationship with Him, experiencing the hope, assurance, and joy that come from knowing the eternal Son of God.

This foundational truth shapes our identity as believers and empowers us to live out our faith with confidence and joy, sharing the hope and life we have found in Jesus with a world in need. Through Jesus, we encounter the divine source of salvation, truth, and life, leading us into a deeper relationship with God and a life of purpose and fulfillment.

Jesus' Pre-Existence and Glory

In John 17:24, Jesus prays, "Father, I want those you have given me to be with me where I am, and to see my glory, the glory you have given me because you loved me before the creation of the world." This verse is part of Jesus' High Priestly Prayer, offered on the night before His crucifixion. It reveals profound aspects of Jesus' divine nature, including His pre-existence, His eternal glory, and the love shared between Him and the Father before the foundation of the world. In this chapter, we will delve into the significance of Jesus' prayer, exploring how it reveals His divine nature and His desire for His followers to share in His glory.

The Context of the Prayer

The High Priestly Prayer

John 17 records Jesus' High Priestly Prayer, a deeply intimate conversation between Jesus and the Father. This prayer is divided into three parts: Jesus prays for Himself (John 17:1-5), for His disciples (John 17:6-19), and for all future believers (John 17:20-26). In this final section, Jesus expresses His desire for unity among His followers and for them to witness His divine glory.

Jesus' Imminent Departure

As Jesus prepares for His imminent departure through His death, resurrection, and ascension, He seeks to reassure His disciples and all future believers of His ongoing presence and the hope of eternal life with Him. His prayer in John 17:24 reveals His deep love for His followers and His desire for them to experience the fullness of His glory.

Jesus' Pre-Existence

"Before the creation of the world."

In John 17:24, Jesus references His existence "before the creation of the world." This statement is a clear assertion of His pre-existence, affirming that Jesus existed with the Father before anything was created. This pre-existence is a fundamental aspect of Jesus' divine nature, setting Him apart from all created beings.

The prologue of John's Gospel reinforces this truth: "In the beginning was the Word, and the Word was with God, and the Word was God. He was with God in the beginning. Through him all things were made; without him nothing was made that has been made" (John 1:1-3). Jesus, the Word, is eternal and co-existent with the Father, participating in the creation of all things.

The Glory of Jesus

The Eternal Glory

Jesus prays that His followers may see His glory, the glory given to Him by the Father. This glory is not a new attribute but something Jesus possessed from eternity. The glory Jesus speaks of is the manifestation of His divine nature, His majesty, and His splendor. It is a glory that reflects His identity as the Son of God, equal with the Father in power and essence.

In the Old Testament, God's glory is often associated with His presence and majesty, as seen in the tabernacle and the temple. For instance, Exodus 40:34-35 describes the glory of the Lord filling the tabernacle. Similarly, Jesus embodies this divine glory, making it visible through His life and ministry.

The Revelation of Glory in the Incarnation

Although Jesus temporarily set aside the full display of His divine glory to become human, His life and works revealed glimpses of this glory. John 1:14 states, "The Word became flesh and made his dwelling among us. We have seen his glory, the glory of the one and only Son, who came from the Father, full of grace and truth."

One of the most significant moments where Jesus' glory was revealed is the Transfiguration. In Matthew 17:1-2, we read, "After six days Jesus took with him Peter, James, and John the brother of James, and led them up a high mountain by themselves. There he was transfigured before them. His face shone like the sun, and his clothes became as white as the light." This event provided the disciples with a glimpse of Jesus' true divine nature and glory.

The Father's Love

"Loved me before the creation of the world."

Jesus' prayer highlights the eternal love shared between Him and the Father. This love is an integral part of the divine relationship within the Trinity. It signifies the deep, unbroken fellowship and mutual affection between the Father and the Son, existing before the foundation of the world.

This eternal love is also the basis for the redemptive plan. In John 3:16, we read, "For God so loved the world that he gave his one and only Son, that whoever believes in him shall not perish but have eternal life." The love that the Father has for the Son overflows to humanity, motivating the mission of Jesus to save and restore.

The Desire for Believers to See His Glory

Sharing in Jesus' Glory

Jesus' prayer expresses His desire for His followers to be with Him and to see His glory. This request reflects His love and longing for intimate fellowship with His people. Jesus wants His followers to experience the fullness of His presence and to witness the divine glory that He shares with the Father.

The apostle Paul echoes this hope in Colossians 3:4, where he writes, "When Christ, who is your life, appears, then you also will appear with him in glory." Believers are invited to share in Jesus' glory, experiencing the ultimate fulfillment of their salvation in His presence.

The Promise of Eternal Life

Jesus' prayer also underscores the promise of eternal life for believers. In John 14:2-3, Jesus assures His disciples, "My Father's house has many rooms; if that were not so, would I have told you that I am going there to prepare a place for you? And if I go and prepare a place for you, I will come back and take you to be with me that you also may be where I am." The ultimate hope for believers is to be with Jesus, beholding His glory and enjoying eternal fellowship with Him.

Theological Implications of Jesus' Pre-Existence and Glory

Affirmation of Jesus' Divinity

Jesus' reference to His pre-existent glory and the love He shared with the Father before the creation of the world is a clear affirmation of His divinity. It establishes that Jesus is not merely a prophet or a great teacher but God Himself, who existed eternally with the Father. This truth is central to Christian theology, underscoring the uniqueness and supremacy of Jesus Christ.

The affirmation of Jesus' divinity also highlights the significance of the Incarnation. The fact that the eternal, glorious Son of God took on human flesh to redeem humanity is a profound mystery and a demonstration of God's incredible love and grace.

The Unity of the Trinity

Jesus' prayer also highlights the unity of the Trinity. The shared glory and love between the Father and the Son point to their essential unity and mutual indwelling. While the distinct persons of the Trinity have different roles in the economy of salvation, they are one in essence and purpose.

This unity is a model for the church. In His prayer, Jesus also prays for the unity of His followers, reflecting the unity He shares with the Father (John 17:21-23). Believers are called to live in unity, reflecting the love and harmony of the Triune God.

The Call to Reflect Jesus' Glory

Living as Reflectors of His Glory

As followers of Christ, we are called to reflect His glory in our lives. This involves living in a way that honors Him and demonstrates His presence in us. In 2 Corinthians 3:18, Paul writes, "And we all, who with unveiled faces contemplate the Lord's glory, are being transformed into his image with ever-increasing glory, which comes from the Lord, who is the Spirit."

This transformation is a process of sanctification, where we grow in Christ-likeness and reflect more of His character and glory. It involves surrendering to the Holy Spirit's work in our lives and allowing Him to shape us into the image of Christ.

Bearing Witness to His Glory

We are also called to bear witness to Jesus' glory in the world. This involves sharing the Gospel, living out our faith with integrity, and demonstrating the love and grace of Christ to others. Our lives should point to the reality of Jesus' divine nature and the hope we have in Him.

In Matthew 5:16, Jesus exhorts His followers, "Let your light shine before others, that they may see your good deeds and glorify your Father in heaven." By reflecting Jesus' glory in our actions and attitudes, we draw others to Him and bring glory to God.

Conclusion

John 17:24 reveals the profound truth of Jesus' divine nature through His prayer, "Father, I want those you have given me to be with me where I am, and to see my glory, the glory you have given me because you loved me before the creation of the world." This statement emphasizes Jesus' pre-existence, His eternal glory, and the deep love shared between Him and the Father. It underscores His divinity and the intimate relationship within the Trinity.

Understanding Jesus' pre-existence and glory deepens our faith and provides a foundation for our hope in eternal life. It calls us to reflect His glory in our lives, living in a way that honors Him and bears witness to His divine nature. As we embrace the truth of Jesus' pre-existence and glory, we are invited into a transformative relationship with Him, experiencing the hope, assurance, and joy that come from knowing the eternal Son of God.

This foundational truth shapes our identity as believers and empowers us to live out our faith with confidence and joy, sharing the hope and life we have found in Jesus with a world in need. Through Jesus, we encounter the divine source of salvation, truth, and life, leading us into a deeper relationship with God and a life of purpose and fulfillment.

141

CHAPTER 06

JESUS AS THE LIFE AND RESURRECTION

In John 11:25-26, Jesus makes a profound declaration to Martha: "I am the resurrection and the life. Whoever believes in me, though he die, yet shall he live, and everyone who lives and believes in me shall never die." This statement is made in the context of the death of Lazarus, one of Jesus' close friends. It reveals the depth of Jesus' divine nature and His power over life and death. This chapter will delve into the significance of Jesus' claim, exploring how it reveals His divine nature and the hope He offers to believers.

The Context of the Declaration

The Death of Lazarus

The backdrop for Jesus' declaration is the death of Lazarus, the brother of Mary and Martha. In John 11, we learn that Lazarus has fallen seriously ill. Despite receiving word of Lazarus' condition, Jesus delays His visit, and Lazarus dies. By the time Jesus arrives in Bethany, Lazarus has been in the tomb for four days, and his sisters are mourning his loss.

Martha's Grief and Faith

When Martha hears that Jesus has arrived, she goes out to meet Him and expresses her sorrow: "Lord, if you had been here, my brother would not have died" (John 11:21). Despite her grief, Martha shows faith in Jesus' power, saying, "But I know that even now God will give you whatever you ask" (John 11:22). It is in this context that Jesus makes His profound declaration about being the resurrection and the life.

Jesus as the Resurrection

"I am the resurrection."

When Jesus declares, "I am the resurrection," He asserts His power over death and His ability to restore life. This statement is a clear assertion of His divine nature, as only God has the power to give life and conquer death. By identifying Himself as the resurrection, Jesus reveals that He holds the keys to life and death.

The Power to Raise the Dead

Throughout His ministry, Jesus demonstrated His power to raise the dead. He raised Jairus' daughter (Mark 5:21-43), the widow's son at Nain (Luke 7:11-17), and ultimately, Lazarus. These miracles are signs of His divine authority and

His role as the giver of life. They foreshadow His own resurrection, which is the cornerstone of Christian faith.

Jesus' resurrection is the ultimate demonstration of His power over death. In 1 Corinthians 15:20-22, Paul writes, "But Christ has indeed been raised from the dead, the firstfruits of those who have fallen asleep. For since death came through a man, the resurrection of the dead comes also through a man. For as in Adam all die, so in Christ all will be made alive." Jesus' victory over death provides the foundation for the hope of resurrection for all believers.

Jesus as the Life

"I am the life."

When Jesus declares, "I am the life," He emphasizes that He is the source of all life, both physical and spiritual. This statement underscores His divine nature as the creator and sustainer of life. In John 1:4, we read, "In him was life, and that life was the light of all mankind." Jesus, as the life, is the source of all that is living and vibrant.

The Source of Eternal Life

Jesus' role as the life is most profoundly demonstrated in His offer of eternal life. In John 10:10, He declares, "I have come that they may have life, and have it to the full." This abundant life is a life characterized by spiritual vitality, purpose, and joy, grounded in a relationship with Jesus.

Jesus' promise of eternal life extends beyond mere existence to a fullness and richness of life that begins now and continues forever. In John 5:24, He says, "Very truly I tell you, whoever hears my word and believes him who sent me has eternal life and will not be judged but has crossed over from death to life." This promise assures believers of their eternal destiny with God.

The Promise of Resurrection and Eternal Life

"Whoever believes in me, though he die, yet shall he live."

Jesus' promise that those who believe in Him will live even though they die provides profound hope and assurance. This statement affirms the reality of physical death but promises a future resurrection and eternal life. Believers can face death with confidence, knowing that it is not the end but a transition to eternal life with Christ.

"Everyone who lives and believes in me shall never die."

Jesus' further promise that those who live and believe in Him shall never die highlights the continuity of eternal life. While physical death may occur, spiritual death is conquered through faith in Jesus. This promise assures believers of their eternal security in Christ, grounded in His victory over sin and death.

Theological Implications of Jesus as the Life and Resurrection

Affirmation of Jesus' Divinity

Jesus' declarations as the resurrection and the life are clear affirmations of His divinity. These statements underscore His unique role as the giver of life and conqueror of death. They highlight His divine authority and power, distinguishing Him as the Son of God who holds the keys to life and death.

The Hope of Eternal Life

The promises of resurrection and eternal life provide a foundation of hope for believers. In 1 Thessalonians 4:13-14, Paul writes, "Brothers and sisters, we do not want you to be uninformed about those who sleep in death, so that you do not grieve like the rest of mankind, who have no hope. For we believe that Jesus died and rose again, and so we believe that God will bring with Jesus those who have fallen asleep in him." The hope of resurrection and eternal life assures believers of their future with Christ and provides comfort in times of loss.

The Call to Faith

Martha's Confession of Faith

In response to Jesus' declaration, Martha makes a profound confession of faith: "Yes, Lord," she replied, "I believe that you are the Messiah, the Son of God, who is to come into the world" (John 11:27). Martha's faith serves as an example for all believers. Despite her grief and the apparent finality of death, she affirms her belief in Jesus' identity and His power to give life.

This confession of faith is a crucial aspect of the Christian response to Jesus' declaration. Believing in Jesus as the resurrection and the life involves trusting in His power, accepting His authority, and relying on His promise of eternal life.

An Invitation to All

Jesus' declaration of the resurrection and life is an invitation to all people to believe in Him. It is a call to place faith in Him as the source of life and the conqueror of death. This invitation extends to everyone, regardless of their background or circumstances. Jesus' offer of life is universal and inclusive, inviting all to experience the hope and assurance He provides.

The Implications for Believers

Living in the Light of the Resurrection

Believing in Jesus as the resurrection and the life has profound implications for how we live. It calls us to live with hope, knowing that death has been conquered and that eternal life awaits us. This hope transforms our perspective on suffering, loss, and the challenges of life, enabling us to face them with faith and confidence in Jesus' promise.

Sharing the Hope of the Resurrection

As followers of Jesus, we are called to share the hope of the resurrection with others. This involves proclaiming the good news of Jesus' victory over death and inviting others to believe in Him. Our witness is a testament to the transformative power of Jesus' life and resurrection, offering hope to a world in need.

Conclusion

John 11:25-26 reveals the profound truth of Jesus' divine nature through His declaration, "I am the resurrection and the life. Whoever believes in me, though he die, yet shall he live, and everyone who lives and believes in me shall never die." This statement emphasizes Jesus' power over life and death and His ability to grant eternal life to all who believe in Him. As the resurrection and the life, Jesus offers hope and assurance, demonstrating His divine authority and fulfilling God's redemptive plan.

Understanding Jesus as the resurrection and the life deepens our faith and provides a foundation for our hope in eternal life. It calls us to believe in Him, live in the light of His resurrection, and share the hope He offers with others. Through Jesus, we encounter the divine source of life, who conquers death and brings us into an everlasting relationship with God. This foundational truth shapes our identity as believers and empowers us to live out our faith with confidence and joy, sharing the hope and life we have found in Jesus with a world in need.

Jesus' Divine Authority

In John 5:19-23, Jesus articulates His divine authority and unity with the Father, stating, "Very truly I tell you, the Son can do nothing by himself; he can do only what he sees his Father doing, because whatever the Father does the Son also does. For the Father loves the Son and shows him all he does. Yes, and he will show him even greater works than these, so that you will be amazed. For just as the Father raises the dead and gives them life, even so the Son gives life to whom he is pleased to give it. Moreover, the Father judges no one, but has entrusted all judgment to the Son, that all may honor the Son just as they honor the Father. Whoever does not honor the Son does not honor the Father, who sent him." This passage provides a profound insight into Jesus' divine nature, authority, and relationship with the Father. This chapter will explore these key aspects, revealing the depth of Jesus' divinity and His unique role in God's redemptive plan.

The Context of the Declaration

Healing at the Pool of Bethesda

The context for Jesus' declaration of divine authority is the healing of a man at the Pool of Bethesda. In John 5:1-15, Jesus heals a man who had been an invalid for thirty-eight years. This miracle, performed on the Sabbath, provokes the Jewish leaders, who question Jesus' authority to heal on the Sabbath and accuse Him of breaking the law.

Jesus' Response to the Jewish Leaders

In response to their accusations, Jesus explains His actions by revealing His unique relationship with the Father and His divine authority. His response goes beyond justifying His actions to making profound theological claims about His identity and mission.

Jesus' Unity with the Father

"The Son can do nothing by himself."

Jesus begins by stating, "Very truly I tell you, the Son can do nothing by himself; he can do only what he sees his Father doing." This statement highlights the intimate and inseparable relationship between Jesus and the Father. It emphasizes Jesus' complete dependence on the Father and His perfect obedience to the Father's will.

Mirroring the Father's Actions

Jesus' declaration that "whatever the Father does the Son also does" underscores His unity with the Father. This unity is not merely in purpose but in action and essence. Jesus' works are a direct reflection of the Father's will and activity. This mirroring of the Father's actions indicates that Jesus operates with divine authority and is fully aligned with the Father's will.

The Father's Love and Revelation

The Father's Love for the Son

Jesus explains that "the Father loves the Son and shows him all he does." This love is the basis for the intimate relationship between the Father and the Son. It is a love that involves complete transparency and mutual understanding. The Father's love for the Son is expressed in revealing His works to Him, ensuring that the Son's actions are a perfect reflection of the Father's will.

Greater Works to Come

Jesus continues, "Yes, and he will show him even greater works than these, so that you will be amazed." This statement points to the ongoing revelation of the Father's works to the Son and the greater miracles that Jesus will perform. These greater works include the raising of the dead and the final judgment, which will further reveal Jesus' divine authority and glorify the Father.

Jesus' Authority to Give Life

Raising the Dead

Jesus declares, "For just as the Father raises the dead and gives them life, even so the Son gives life to whom he is pleased to give it." This statement emphasizes Jesus' divine authority to grant life, a power traditionally attributed to God alone. By claiming this authority, Jesus asserts His divinity and His role in giving both physical and spiritual life.

The Giver of Eternal Life

Jesus' authority to give life extends beyond physical resurrection to the granting of eternal life. In John 5:24, He states, "Very truly I tell you, whoever hears my word and believes him who sent me has eternal life and will not be judged but has crossed over from death to life." Jesus' words offer the promise of eternal life to those who believe in Him, underscoring His role as the source of life and salvation.

Jesus' Authority to Judge

Entrusted with Judgment

Jesus reveals that "the Father judges no one, but has entrusted all judgment to the Son." This delegation of judgment to Jesus signifies His divine authority and His role as the final arbiter of human destiny. Judgment, a divine prerogative, is now exercised by Jesus, highlighting His equality with the Father.

Honoring the Son

The purpose of entrusting judgment to the Son is "that all may honor the Son just as they honor the Father." Jesus' authority to judge ensures that He receives the same honor and reverence as the Father. This honor is due to His divine nature and His role in executing God's justice and mercy.

Theological Implications of Jesus' Divine Authority

Affirmation of Jesus' Divinity

Jesus' statements in John 5:19-23 are clear affirmations of His divinity. His unity with the Father, His authority to give life, and His role as judge all point to His divine nature. These declarations establish that Jesus is not merely a prophet or teacher but God incarnate, possessing all the attributes and authority of deity.

The Relationship Within the Trinity

The passage also highlights the relationship within the Trinity. The mutual love, revelation, and honor between the Father and the Son illustrate the unity and distinct roles within the Godhead. This relationship serves as a model for understanding the divine nature and the cooperative work of the Father, Son, and Holy Spirit in the plan of salvation.

The Call to Honor the Son

Recognizing Jesus' Authority

Believers are called to recognize and honor Jesus' divine authority. This involves acknowledging His unique role as the giver of life and the judge of all humanity. It also means submitting to His teachings and living in accordance with His will.

Living in Obedience to Jesus

Honoring Jesus' authority requires living in obedience to His commands. In John 14:15, Jesus says, "If you love me, keep my commands." Obedience to Jesus is a reflection of our recognition of His divine authority and our commitment to following Him as Lord and Savior.

The Hope of Eternal Life

Assurance of Salvation

Jesus' authority to give life provides believers with the assurance of salvation. His promise of eternal life to those who believe in Him offers hope and security, knowing that our destiny is in the hands of the one who holds all authority. In John 10:28, Jesus assures us, "I give them eternal life, and they shall never perish; no one will snatch them out of my hand."

The Promise of Resurrection

Jesus' authority over life and death also assures us of the promise of resurrection. In John 6:40, He declares, "For my Father's will is that everyone who looks to the Son and believes in him shall have eternal life, and I will raise them up at the last day." This promise of resurrection and eternal life is a cornerstone of Christian hope, providing comfort and encouragement in the face of death.

Conclusion

John 5:19-23 reveals the profound truth of Jesus' divine nature through His declaration of unity with the Father, His authority to give life, and His role as judge. These statements emphasize Jesus' divinity, His unique relationship with the Father, and His integral role in God's redemptive plan. Understanding Jesus' divine authority deepens our faith and provides a foundation for our hope in eternal life.

As we embrace the truth of Jesus' divine authority, we are called to honor Him, live in obedience to His commands, and share the hope of eternal life with others. Through Jesus, we encounter the divine source of life and salvation, leading us into a deeper relationship with God and a life of purpose and fulfillment. This foundational truth shapes our identity as believers and empowers us to live out our faith with confidence and joy, sharing the hope and life we have found in Jesus with a world in need.

CHAPTER 07

JESUS' DIVINE AUTHORITY

In John 5:24-27, Jesus speaks of His divine authority to give eternal life and execute judgment, declaring, "Very truly I tell you, whoever hears my word and believes him who sent me has eternal life and will not be judged but has crossed over from death to life. Very truly I tell you, a time is coming and has now come when the dead will hear the voice of the Son of God and those who hear will live. For as the Father has life in himself, so he has granted the Son also to have life in himself. And he has given him authority to judge because he is the Son of Man." This passage reveals profound truths about Jesus' divine nature, His role as the giver of life, and His authority to judge. In this chapter, we will explore these aspects, uncovering the depth of Jesus' divinity and His unique position within God's redemptive plan.

The Context of the Declaration

Healing at the Pool of Bethesda

The backdrop for Jesus' declaration is the healing of a man at the Pool of Bethesda. In John 5:1-15, Jesus heals a man who had been an invalid for thirty-eight years. This miracle, performed on the Sabbath, provokes the Jewish leaders, who question Jesus' authority to heal on the Sabbath and accuse Him of breaking the law.

Jesus' Response to the Jewish Leaders

In response to their accusations, Jesus explains His actions by revealing His unique relationship with the Father and His divine authority. His response goes beyond justifying His actions to making profound theological claims about His identity and mission.

Jesus' Authority to Give Eternal Life

"Whoever hears my word and believes him who sent me has eternal life."

Jesus begins by emphasizing the importance of hearing and believing His word. He states that those who hear His word and believe in the Father who sent Him have eternal life. This statement underscores the necessity of faith in Jesus for obtaining eternal life. It highlights the centrality of Jesus' teachings and the necessity of believing in Him as the Son of God.

This assurance of eternal life is immediate. Jesus declares that those who believe have already "crossed over from death to life." This transition from spiritual death to eternal life occurs at the moment of faith in Jesus, offering believers the promise of eternal life in the present and future.

The Power to Raise the Dead

"A time is coming and has now come when the dead will hear the voice of the Son of God and those who hear will live."

Jesus asserts His authority to give life to the dead. This statement has both a present and future dimension. In the present, Jesus' words have the power to bring spiritual life to those who are spiritually dead. Those who hear His voice and believe are granted eternal life.

In the future, Jesus' authority extends to the physical resurrection of the dead. He speaks of a time when the dead will hear His voice and rise from their graves. This power to raise the dead is a clear demonstration of His divine authority and His role as the giver of life.

The Son of God and Life in Himself

Jesus explains the basis of His authority to give life: "For as the Father has life in himself, so he has granted the Son also to have life in himself." This statement reveals the unique relationship between the Father and the Son. Just as the Father possesses life in Himself, so does the Son. This self-existent life is a defining attribute of divinity, emphasizing Jesus' divine nature.

Having life in Himself means that Jesus is the source of all life. He is not dependent on anything or anyone for His existence. This intrinsic life allows Him to give life to others, both spiritually and physically.

Jesus' Authority to Judge

"He has given him authority to judge because he is the Son of Man."

In addition to His authority to give life, Jesus has been granted the authority to judge. This judgment is a divine prerogative, highlighting Jesus' unique role within the Godhead. The Father has entrusted all judgment to the Son, indicating the complete confidence and unity between the Father and the Son.

The title "Son of Man" is significant. It is a messianic title from the Old Testament, particularly from Daniel 7:13-14, where the Son of Man is given authority, glory, and sovereign power. By referring to Himself as the Son of Man, Jesus identifies with this prophetic figure, emphasizing His divine authority and His role in executing God's judgment.

Theological Implications of Jesus' Divine Authority

Affirmation of Jesus' Divinity

Jesus' statements in John 5:24-27 are clear affirmations of His divinity. His authority to give life and to judge are attributes of God alone. These declarations establish that Jesus is not merely a prophet or teacher but God incarnate, possessing all the attributes and authority of a deity.

The Relationship Within the Trinity

The passage also highlights the relationship within the Trinity. The Father granting the Son authority to give life and judge illustrates the unity and distinct roles within the Godhead. This relationship serves as a model for understanding the divine nature and the cooperative work of the Father, Son, and Holy Spirit in the plan of salvation.

The Assurance of Eternal Life

Immediate Assurance

Jesus' promise that those who believe have already crossed over from death to life provides immediate assurance to believers. This assurance is not based on future events but on present faith in Jesus. Believers can have confidence in their eternal destiny, knowing that they have already received the gift of eternal life through faith in Christ.

The Hope of Resurrection

Jesus' authority to raise the dead also provides hope for the future resurrection. Believers can look forward to the day when they will hear the voice of the Son of God and rise from their graves to eternal life. This hope of resurrection offers comfort and encouragement in the face of death, knowing that it is not the end but a transition to eternal life with Christ.

The Call to Honor the Son

Recognizing Jesus' Authority

Believers are called to recognize and honor Jesus' divine authority. This involves acknowledging His unique role as the giver of life and the judge of all humanity. It also means submitting to His teachings and living in accordance with His will.

Living in Obedience to Jesus

Honoring Jesus' authority requires living in obedience to His commands. In John 14:15, Jesus says, "If you love me, keep my commands." Obedience to Jesus is a reflection of our recognition of His divine authority and our commitment to following Him as Lord and Savior.

The Implications for Believers

Living in the Light of Jesus' Authority

Believing in Jesus' authority to give life and judge has profound implications for how we live. It calls us to live with the assurance of eternal life and the hope of resurrection. This assurance transforms our perspective on suffering, loss, and the challenges of life, enabling us to face them with faith and confidence in Jesus' promise.

Sharing the Hope of Eternal Life

As followers of Jesus, we are called to share the hope of eternal life with others. This involves proclaiming the good news of Jesus' victory over death and His authority to give life. Our witness is a testament to the transformative power of Jesus' life and resurrection, offering hope to a world in need.

Conclusion

John 5:24-27 reveals the profound truth of Jesus' divine nature through His declaration of authority to give eternal life and execute judgment. These statements emphasize Jesus' divinity, His unique relationship with the Father, and His integral role in God's redemptive plan. Understanding Jesus' divine authority deepens our faith and provides a foundation for our hope in eternal life.

As we embrace the truth of Jesus' divine authority, we are called to honor Him, live in obedience to His commands, and share the hope of eternal life with others. Through Jesus, we encounter the divine source of life and salvation, leading us into a deeper relationship with God and a life of purpose and fulfillment. This foundational truth shapes our identity as believers and empowers us to live out our faith with confidence and joy, sharing the hope and life we have found in Jesus with a world in need.

CHAPTER 08

THE TESTIMONIES OF JESUS' DIVINITY

In John 5:31-36, Jesus speaks about the testimonies that confirm His divine nature. He lists the testimony of John the Baptist and the works He performs as evidence of His identity as the Son of God. This chapter will delve into the significance of these testimonies, exploring how they reveal Jesus' divine nature and affirm His mission.

The Context of the Declaration

The Healing at Bethesda

The backdrop for Jesus' discussion on testimonies is the healing of a man at the Pool of Bethesda. After this miracle, Jesus faces opposition from the Jewish leaders who question His authority and accuse Him of breaking the Sabbath. In response, Jesus provides a series of declarations about His relationship with the Father and His divine mission.

The Importance of Testimony

In Jewish law, the testimony of multiple witnesses was required to establish the truth of a matter. In Deuteronomy 19:15, it is stated, "A matter must be established by the testimony of two or three witnesses." Jesus appeals to this principle by presenting several witnesses that testify to His divine nature.

The Testimony of Jesus

Self-Testimony

Jesus begins by acknowledging that if He were to testify about Himself, His testimony would not be valid in the eyes of the law: "If I testify about myself, my testimony is not true" (John 5:31). This does not mean that His self-testimony is false, but rather that He recognizes the need for external witnesses to validate His claims according to Jewish law.

The Testimony of John the Baptist

John as a Witness

Jesus points to John the Baptist as a significant witness to His divine nature: "There is another who testifies in my favor, and I know that his testimony about me is true. You have sent to John and he has testified to the truth" (John 5:32-33). John the Baptist's role was to prepare the way for the Messiah and to bear witness to Him.

John's Testimony

John the Baptist's testimony about Jesus is recorded in John 1:29-34. When he saw Jesus coming toward him, he declared, "Look, the Lamb of God, who takes away the sin of the world! This is the one I meant when I said, 'A man who comes after me has surpassed me because he was before me.'" John also testified that he saw the Spirit descend on Jesus like a dove and remain on Him, confirming that Jesus is the Son of God.

The Significance of John's Testimony

John's testimony is significant because he was a respected prophet recognized by the Jewish leaders and the people. His witness adds credibility to Jesus' claims and highlights the fulfillment of Old Testament prophecies concerning the Messiah.

The Testimony of Jesus' Works

The Works as Evidence

Jesus presents His miraculous works as further testimony to His divine nature: "I have testimony weightier than that of John. For the works that the Father has given me to finish—the very works that I am doing—testify that the Father has sent me" (John 5:36). The miracles Jesus performed were not merely acts of compassion but signs that pointed to His divine authority and identity.

Miracles as Signs

Throughout the Gospel of John, Jesus' miracles are referred to as signs that reveal His glory and divine nature. These include turning water into wine at Cana (John 2:1-11), healing the nobleman's son (John 4:46-54), feeding the five thousand (John 6:1-14), walking on water (John 6:16-21), healing the blind man (John 9:1-12), and raising Lazarus from the dead (John 11:1-44).

Each of these miracles serves as a testament to Jesus' authority over nature, illness, and even death. They demonstrate His power and confirm that He is indeed sent by the Father.

The Testimony of the Father

The Father's Witness

Jesus also refers to the testimony of the Father: "And the Father who sent me has himself testified concerning me. You have never heard his voice nor seen his form, nor does his word dwell in you, for you do not believe the one he sent" (John 5:37-38). The Father's testimony is paramount, as it comes directly from God.

The Baptism and Transfiguration

The Father's testimony is explicitly recorded at Jesus' baptism and the Transfiguration. At His baptism, a voice from heaven said, "This is my Son, whom I love; with him I am well pleased" (Matthew 3:17). At the Transfiguration, the

Father again declares, "This is my Son, whom I love; with him I am well pleased. Listen to him!" (Matthew 17:5).

These divine affirmations confirm Jesus' identity and mission, leaving no doubt about His divine nature.

The Testimony of the Scriptures

The Scriptures Point to Jesus

Jesus points out that the Scriptures themselves testify about Him: "You study the Scriptures diligently because you think that in them you have eternal life. These are the very Scriptures that testify about me" (John 5:39). The Old Testament writings contain numerous prophecies and types that point to the coming Messiah, all of which find their fulfillment in Jesus.

Fulfillment of Prophecy

The life, death, and resurrection of Jesus fulfill many Old Testament prophecies. For instance, Isaiah 53 describes the suffering servant who would bear the sins of many, and Psalm 22 vividly portrays the crucifixion. These fulfillments serve as powerful testimonies to Jesus' divine nature and mission.

Theological Implications of the Testimonies

Affirmation of Jesus' Divinity

The combined testimonies of John the Baptist, Jesus' works, the Father, and the Scriptures provide a compelling case for Jesus' divinity. They affirm that Jesus is the Son of God, sent by the Father to accomplish the work of salvation.

The Necessity of Faith

These testimonies call for a response of faith. Jesus' statements and the corroborating witnesses demand that we recognize and believe in Him as the Messiah and the Son of God. Faith in Jesus is essential for receiving the eternal life He offers.

The Call to Believe

Believing the Witnesses

Believers are called to accept the testimonies about Jesus and place their faith in Him. The evidence provided by these witnesses is not only for intellectual assent but for a transformative faith that trusts in Jesus for salvation and follows Him as Lord.

Living Out Our Faith

Faith in Jesus should lead to a life of obedience and discipleship. As we believe in the testimonies of His divinity, we are called to live in a manner that reflects His teachings and demonstrates our commitment to Him. This involves following His commands, loving others, and proclaiming the Gospel.

Conclusion

John 5:31-36 presents a powerful case for Jesus' divine nature through the testimonies of John the Baptist, Jesus' works, the Father, and the Scriptures. These witnesses collectively affirm that Jesus is the Son of God, sent by the Father to bring salvation to the world. Understanding these testimonies deepens our faith and provides a solid foundation for our belief in Jesus' divinity.

As we embrace the truth of these testimonies, we are called to respond with faith, recognizing Jesus as the Messiah and the Son of God. This faith transforms our lives, leading us to live in obedience to His commands and to share the hope of salvation with others. Through Jesus, we encounter the divine source of life and truth, leading us into a deeper relationship with God and a life of purpose and fulfillment. This foundational truth shapes our identity as believers and empowers us to live out our faith with confidence and joy, sharing the hope and life we have found in Jesus with a world in need.

The Testimonies of Jesus' Divinity

In John 5:37-40, Jesus presents two significant testimonies to His divine nature: the testimony of the Father and the testimony of the Scriptures. He declares that the Father Himself has testified about Him, and that the Scriptures point to Him as the source of eternal life. This chapter will delve into these testimonies, exploring how they reveal Jesus' divine nature and affirm His mission.

The Context of the Declaration

Healing at the Pool of Bethesda

The context for Jesus' declaration is the healing of a man at the Pool of Bethesda. After this miracle, Jesus faces opposition from the Jewish leaders who question His authority and accuse Him of breaking the Sabbath. In response, Jesus provides a series of declarations about His relationship with the Father and His divine mission.

The Importance of Testimony

In Jewish law, the testimony of multiple witnesses was required to establish the truth of a matter. In Deuteronomy 19:15, it is stated, "A matter must be established by the testimony of two or three witnesses." Jesus appeals to this principle by presenting several witnesses that testify to His divine nature.

The Testimony of the Father

"And the Father who sent me has himself testified concerning me."

Jesus begins by emphasizing the testimony of the Father: "And the Father who sent me has himself testified concerning me" (John 5:37). This statement underscores the importance and credibility of the Father's testimony. The

Father's witness is paramount because it comes directly from God, the ultimate authority.

The Father's Testimony at Baptism and Transfiguration

The Father's testimony is explicitly recorded at Jesus' baptism and the Transfiguration. At His baptism, a voice from heaven said, "This is my Son, whom I love; with him I am well pleased" (Matthew 3:17). At the Transfiguration, the Father again declares, "This is my Son, whom I love; with him I am well pleased. Listen to him!" (Matthew 17:5).

These divine affirmations confirm Jesus' identity and mission, leaving no doubt about His divine nature. They reveal the special relationship between the Father and the Son, highlighting Jesus as the chosen one sent to accomplish God's redemptive plan.

The Father's Ongoing Witness

In addition to these specific events, the Father's ongoing witness is seen in the works Jesus performs. In John 5:36, Jesus states, "For the works that the Father has given me to finish—the very works that I am doing—testify that the Father has sent me." The miracles and teachings of Jesus are direct evidence of the Father's endorsement and support.

The Testimony of the Scriptures

"These are the very Scriptures that testify about me."

Jesus points out that the Scriptures themselves testify about Him: "You study the Scriptures diligently because you think that in them you have eternal life. These are the very Scriptures that testify about me" (John 5:39). The Old Testament writings contain numerous prophecies and types that point to the coming Messiah, all of which find their fulfillment in Jesus.

Fulfillment of Prophecy

The life, death, and resurrection of Jesus fulfill many Old Testament prophecies. For instance, Isaiah 53 describes the suffering servant who would bear the sins of many, and Psalm 22 vividly portrays the crucifixion. These fulfillments serve as powerful testimonies to Jesus' divine nature and mission.

Other significant prophecies include:

- Micah 5:2 - Foretelling the Messiah's birth in Bethlehem.

- Isaiah 7:14 - Predicting the virgin birth.

- Zechariah 9:9 - Prophesying the triumphal entry.

- Psalm 16:10 - Declaring the resurrection.

These prophecies, written centuries before Jesus' birth, point unmistakably to Him and confirm His identity as the Messiah.

The Rejection of Testimonies

Unbelief Despite Evidence

Despite the compelling testimonies of the Father and the Scriptures, Jesus confronts the Jewish leaders for their unbelief: "You have never heard his voice nor seen his form, nor does his word dwell in you, for you do not believe the one he sent" (John 5:37-38). Their failure to recognize and accept the testimonies reveals their spiritual blindness and hardness of heart.

Seeking Eternal Life Apart from Jesus

Jesus further critiques their reliance on the Scriptures for eternal life while rejecting Him: "You study the Scriptures diligently because you think that in them you have eternal life. These are the very Scriptures that testify about me, yet you refuse to come to me to have life" (John 5:39-40). Their meticulous study of the Scriptures is in vain because they miss the central message—the testimony about Jesus as the source of eternal life.

Theological Implications of the Testimonies

Affirmation of Jesus' Divinity

The combined testimonies of the Father and the Scriptures provide a compelling case for Jesus' divinity. They affirm that Jesus is the Son of God, sent by the Father to accomplish the work of salvation. These testimonies underscore Jesus' unique identity and divine authority.

The Necessity of Faith

These testimonies call for a response of faith. Jesus' statements and the corroborating witnesses demand that we recognize and believe in Him as the Messiah and the Son of God. Faith in Jesus is essential for receiving the eternal life He offers.

The Call to Believe

Recognizing the Testimonies

Believers are called to recognize and accept the testimonies about Jesus. The evidence provided by the Father and the Scriptures is not only for intellectual assent but for a transformative faith that trusts in Jesus for salvation and follows Him as Lord.

Living Out Our Faith

Faith in Jesus should lead to a life of obedience and discipleship. As we believe in the testimonies of His divinity, we are called to live in a manner that reflects His teachings and demonstrates our commitment to Him. This involves following His commands, loving others, and proclaiming the Gospel.

The Implications for Believers

Living in the Light of Jesus' Authority

Believing in Jesus' divine authority has profound implications for how we live. It calls us to live with the assurance of eternal life and the hope of resurrection. This assurance transforms our perspective on suffering, loss, and the challenges of life, enabling us to face them with faith and confidence in Jesus' promise.

Sharing the Hope of Eternal Life

As followers of Jesus, we are called to share the hope of eternal life with others. This involves proclaiming the good news of Jesus' victory over death and His authority to give life. Our witness is a testament to the transformative power of Jesus' life and resurrection, offering hope to a world in need.

Conclusion

John 5:37-40 presents a powerful case for Jesus' divine nature through the testimonies of the Father and the Scriptures. These witnesses collectively affirm that Jesus is the Son of God, sent by the Father to bring salvation to the world. Understanding these testimonies deepens our faith and provides a solid foundation for our belief in Jesus' divinity.

As we embrace the truth of these testimonies, we are called to respond with faith, recognizing Jesus as the Messiah and the Son of God. This faith transforms our lives, leading us to live in obedience to His commands and to share the hope of salvation with others. Through Jesus, we encounter the divine source of life and truth, leading us into a deeper relationship with God and a life of purpose and fulfillment. This foundational truth shapes our identity as believers and empowers us to live out our faith with confidence and joy, sharing the hope and life we have found in Jesus with a world in need.

CHAPTER 09

JESUS AS THE SOURCE OF ETERNAL LIFE

In John 6:35-40, Jesus makes a profound declaration about His identity and mission: "I am the bread of life. Whoever comes to me will never go hungry, and whoever believes in me will never be thirsty. But as I told you, you have seen me and still you do not believe. All those the Father gives me will come to me, and whoever comes to me I will never drive away. For I have come down from heaven not to do my will but to do the will of him who sent me. And this is the will of him who sent me, that I shall lose none of all those he has given me, but raise them up at the last day. For my Father's will is that everyone who looks to the Son and believes in him shall have eternal life, and I will raise them up at the last day." This passage highlights Jesus' divine nature and His role as the source of eternal life. This chapter will delve into these profound truths, exploring how they reveal Jesus' divinity and the promise of eternal life for those who believe in Him.

The Context of the Declaration

The Feeding of the Five Thousand

The backdrop for Jesus' declaration is the miraculous feeding of the five thousand, an event recorded in John 6:1-15. Jesus multiplies five loaves and two fish to feed a large crowd, demonstrating His divine power and compassion. This miracle sets the stage for His subsequent teaching about the true bread from heaven.

The Crowd's Search for Jesus

After the feeding, the crowd seeks out Jesus, hoping for more miraculous signs and physical sustenance. They find Him on the other side of the Sea of Galilee, and Jesus takes this opportunity to teach them about the spiritual sustenance He offers.

Jesus as the Bread of Life

"I am the bread of life."

When Jesus declares, "I am the bread of life," He is making a profound statement about His divine identity and mission. This declaration is the first of the seven "I Am" statements in the Gospel of John, each of which reveals a different aspect of His divine nature and His relationship with humanity.

The metaphor of bread is rich with meaning. Bread was a staple food in the ancient Near East, essential for physical sustenance and survival. By identifying Himself as the bread of life, Jesus claims to be essential for spiritual sustenance and eternal life. Just as physical bread sustains the body, Jesus, the bread of life, sustains the soul.

Spiritual Nourishment

Jesus promises that those who come to Him will never go hungry, and those who believe in Him will never be thirsty. This promise emphasizes the sufficiency and completeness of the spiritual nourishment He provides. To come to Jesus and believe in Him is to receive the sustenance that satisfies the deepest spiritual hunger and thirst.

This spiritual nourishment is not a one-time event but an ongoing relationship with Jesus. Believers are called to continually come to Him, drawing from His inexhaustible resources of grace, truth, and life. This ongoing relationship is central to the Christian faith, as it sustains and empowers believers to live according to God's will.

The Promise of Eternal Life

"Everyone who looks to the Son and believes in him shall have eternal life."

Jesus' declaration emphasizes the promise of eternal life for those who believe in Him. In John 6:40, He states,

"For my Father's will is that everyone who looks to the Son and believes in him shall have eternal life, and I will raise them up at the last day." Eternal life is not merely an extension of physical existence but a new quality of life characterized by an intimate relationship with God, beginning now and continuing forever.

This promise of eternal life is grounded in Jesus' divine authority and power. As the bread of life, He has the power to grant eternal life and to raise believers from the dead, ensuring that they share in His resurrection and glory.

The Assurance of Salvation

Jesus' words offer profound assurance to believers. In John 6:37, He promises, "All those the Father gives me will come to me, and whoever comes to me I will never drive away." This assurance underscores the security of those who come to Jesus in faith. He will never reject or abandon them, but will keep them safe and secure in His care.

Furthermore, Jesus affirms that He will lose none of those the Father has given Him, but will raise them up at the last day. This promise provides a foundation for the believer's hope, assuring them of their ultimate destiny with God.

The Divine Nature of Jesus

Sent from Heaven

Jesus' declaration, "For I have come down from heaven not to do my will but to do the will of him who sent me," highlights His divine origin and mission. This statement underscores that Jesus is not merely a human teacher or prophet, but the Son of God sent from heaven to accomplish the Father's will.

This divine mission is central to Jesus' identity and authority. Throughout the Gospel of John, Jesus repeatedly emphasizes His unique relationship with the Father and His role as the one sent to reveal God's truth and bring salvation to humanity.

The Giver of Life

Jesus' role as the bread of life and the giver of eternal life underscores His divine nature. In John 1:4, we read, "In him was life, and that life was the light of all mankind." Jesus, as the source of all life, possesses the power to grant eternal life to those who believe in Him.

This divine attribute is further highlighted in Jesus' ability to raise the dead. In John 6:39-40, He promises to raise up believers at the last day, demonstrating His authority over life and death. This power to give life and conquer death is a clear indication of His divinity.

The Call to Faith

Believing in Jesus

Jesus' declaration calls for a response of faith. He invites all people to come to Him and believe in Him as the bread of life. This faith involves recognizing Jesus as the source of spiritual nourishment and eternal life, trusting in His promises, and committing to follow Him.

In John 6:29, Jesus says, "The work of God is this: to believe in the one he has sent." Faith in Jesus is the essential requirement for receiving the eternal life He offers. It is through faith that believers enter into a relationship with Him, experiencing the fullness of His grace and truth.

Living in the Light of Eternal Life

Believing in Jesus as the bread of life has profound implications for how we live. It calls us to live with the assurance of eternal life and the hope of resurrection. This assurance transforms our perspective on suffering, loss, and the challenges of life, enabling us to face them with faith and confidence in Jesus' promise.

Living in the light of eternal life also involves participating in the life of Christ. As we draw near to Him and abide in His presence, we experience His transforming power and become more like Him. This ongoing relationship with Jesus is the source of spiritual vitality and growth.

The Implications for Believers

Spiritual Sustenance

Believing in Jesus as the bread of life means continually seeking Him for spiritual sustenance. This involves regular prayer, reading and meditating on His Word, and living in obedience to His commands. As we draw from His resources, we find the strength and nourishment needed to live according to God's will.

Sharing the Bread of Life

As followers of Jesus, we are called to share the bread of life with others. This involves proclaiming the good news of Jesus' offer of eternal life and inviting others to come to Him in faith. Our witness is a testament to the transformative power of Jesus' life and resurrection, offering hope to a world in need.

Conclusion

John 6:35-40 reveals the profound truth of Jesus' divine nature through His declaration, "I am the bread of life." This statement emphasizes His role as the source of spiritual sustenance and eternal life, highlighting His unique identity and mission. Understanding Jesus as the bread of life deepens our faith and provides a foundation for our hope in eternal life.

As we embrace Jesus' declaration, we are invited into a transformative relationship with Him, experiencing the fullness of His grace and truth. This relationship sustains and empowers us, enabling us to live out our faith with confidence and joy. Through Jesus, we encounter the divine source of life, who satisfies our deepest spiritual hunger and offers the promise of eternal life.

This foundational truth shapes our identity as believers and calls us to share the hope and life we have found in Jesus with a world in need. By living in the light of His promise and drawing near to Him, we experience the abundant life He offers and become conduits of His grace to others.

Jesus as the Source of Eternal Life

In John 6:68-69, Simon Peter makes a profound confession of faith, acknowledging Jesus as the Holy One of God who has the words of eternal life: "Simon Peter answered him, 'Lord, to whom shall we go? You have the words of eternal life. We have come to believe and to know that you are the Holy One of God.'" This declaration comes after many of Jesus' followers turn away, unable to accept His teachings. Peter's confession highlights the recognition of Jesus' divine nature and His unique role as the source of eternal life. In this chapter, we will delve into the significance of Peter's confession, exploring how it reveals Jesus' divinity and the hope He offers to believers.

The Context of the Declaration

The Bread of Life Discourse

The context for Peter's confession is the Bread of Life discourse in John 6. After feeding the five thousand, Jesus teaches the crowd about the true bread from heaven, explaining that He is the bread of life and that those who come to Him will never go hungry or thirsty. He emphasizes the necessity of believing in Him and partaking in His flesh and blood to have eternal life.

The Reaction of the Disciples

Jesus' teaching is difficult for many to accept. In John 6:60, many of His disciples say, "This is a hard teaching. Who can accept it?" As a result, many turn back and no longer follow Him. Jesus then turns to the Twelve and asks, "You do not want to leave too, do you?" (John 6:67).

Peter's Confession of Faith

"Lord, to whom shall we go?"

In response to Jesus' question, Simon Peter speaks for the Twelve, expressing their commitment to Jesus despite the difficult teaching: "Lord, to whom shall we go? You have the words of eternal life" (John 6:68). Peter's rhetorical question highlights the unique position of Jesus. There is no one else who can offer what Jesus offers—eternal life. This acknowledgment underscores the disciples' recognition of

Jesus' unique authority and the life-giving power of His words.

"You have the words of eternal life."

Peter's declaration, "You have the words of eternal life," emphasizes the life-giving nature of Jesus' teachings. Throughout His ministry, Jesus speaks words that bring life, hope, and salvation. His teachings reveal the truth about God, the kingdom of heaven, and the path to eternal life. By recognizing that Jesus' words are the source of eternal life, Peter affirms the transformative power of Jesus' message and His divine authority.

Jesus as the Holy One of God

"We have come to believe and to know that you are the Holy One of God."

Peter's confession continues with a powerful affirmation of Jesus' divine identity: "We have come to believe and to know that you are the Holy One of God" (John 6:69). This title, "the Holy One of God," signifies Jesus' unique status and divine nature. It acknowledges His consecration and set-apartness for God's purposes.

The Significance of the Title

The title "Holy One of God" is rich with theological significance. In the Old Testament, holiness is a defining attribute of God. To be holy is to be set apart, pure, and consecrated. By calling Jesus the Holy One of God, Peter recognizes Him as being uniquely set apart for God's redemptive mission. This title underscores Jesus' divinity and His intimate relationship with the Father.

Old Testament Fulfillment

The acknowledgment of Jesus as the Holy One of God also points to the fulfillment of Old Testament prophecies. Throughout the Old Testament, the Messiah is described as one who is holy and anointed by God. For example, Psalm 16:10 says, "Because you will not abandon me to the realm of the dead, nor will you let your faithful one see decay." This verse is often interpreted as a prophecy about the Messiah's resurrection, highlighting His holiness and divine nature.

The Divine Nature of Jesus

The Source of Eternal Life

Peter's confession that Jesus has the words of eternal life emphasizes Jesus' role as the source of eternal life. Throughout the Gospel of John, Jesus consistently presents Himself as the giver of life. In John 5:24, He states, "Very truly I tell you, whoever hears my word and believes him who sent me has eternal life and will not be judged but has crossed over from death to life."

Jesus' ability to grant eternal life underscores His divine nature. Only God can give life, and by claiming this ability, Jesus reveals His identity as God incarnate. His words are not just teachings but life-giving truths that transform and renew those who believe in Him.

The Unique Relationship with the Father

Peter's acknowledgment of Jesus as the Holy One of God also highlights Jesus' unique relationship with the Father. In John 10:30, Jesus declares, "I and the Father are one." This unity with the Father is essential to understanding Jesus' divine nature. He is not merely a messenger but shares in the divine essence and mission of the Father.

This unique relationship is further emphasized in Jesus' mission to do the Father's will. In John 6:38, Jesus says, "For I have come down from heaven not to do my will but to do the will of him who sent me." Jesus' obedience to the Father and His fulfillment of the Father's redemptive plan highlight His divinity and His role as the mediator between God and humanity.

The Call to Faith

The Necessity of Belief

Peter's confession underscores the necessity of faith in Jesus for receiving eternal life. By acknowledging Jesus as the Holy One of God and the source of eternal life, Peter demonstrates the kind of faith that Jesus calls for. This faith involves recognizing Jesus' divine identity, trusting in His words, and committing to follow Him.

In John 6:29, Jesus explains, "The work of God is this: to believe in the one he has sent." Faith in Jesus is the essential requirement for entering into a relationship with Him and receiving the eternal life He offers. It is through faith that believers experience the transformative power of Jesus' words and the hope of eternal life.

Living Out Our Faith

Faith in Jesus should lead to a life of obedience and discipleship. As we believe in the testimonies of His divinity, we are called to live in a manner that reflects His teachings and demonstrates our commitment to Him. This involves following His commands, loving others, and proclaiming the Gospel.

Living out our faith also means relying on Jesus as the source of spiritual nourishment. Just as physical bread sustains the body, Jesus, the bread of life, sustains the soul. Believers are called to continually come to Jesus, drawing from His inexhaustible resources of grace, truth, and life.

The Implications for Believers

Assurance of Salvation

Peter's confession provides assurance of salvation for believers. By acknowledging Jesus as the Holy One of God and the source of eternal life, believers can have confidence in their eternal destiny. Jesus promises that those who come to Him will never be driven away and that He will raise them up at the last day (John 6:37, 40).

This assurance transforms our perspective on suffering, loss, and the challenges of life, enabling us to face them with faith and confidence in Jesus' promise. The hope of eternal life provides comfort and encouragement, knowing that our ultimate destiny is secure in Christ.

Sharing the Hope of Eternal Life

As followers of Jesus, we are called to share the hope of eternal life with others. This involves proclaiming the good news of Jesus' victory over death and His authority to give life. Our witness is a testament to the transformative power of Jesus' life and resurrection, offering hope to a world in need.

Conclusion

John 6:68-69 reveals the profound truth of Jesus' divine nature through Peter's confession: "Lord, to whom shall we go? You have the words of eternal life. We have come to believe and to know that you are the Holy One of God." This declaration emphasizes Jesus' role as the source of eternal life and highlights His unique identity as the Holy One of God. Understanding Jesus as the source of eternal life deepens our faith and provides a foundation for our hope in eternal life.

As we embrace Peter's confession, we are invited into a transformative relationship with Jesus, experiencing the fullness of His grace and truth. This relationship sustains and empowers us, enabling us to live out our faith with confidence and joy. Through Jesus, we encounter the divine source of life, who satisfies our deepest spiritual hunger and offers the promise of eternal life.

This foundational truth shapes our identity as believers and calls us to share the hope and life we have found in Jesus with a world in need. By living in the light of His promise and drawing near to Him, we experience the abundant life He offers and become conduits of His grace to others.

CHAPTER 10

JESUS' MIRACLES AS SIGN OF HIS DIVINITY

In John 2:1-11, we read about Jesus' first recorded miracle, the turning of water into wine at the wedding in Cana. This miracle, performed early in His public ministry, serves as a profound demonstration of His divine authority over nature. The event is not only a remarkable display of power but also a significant sign that reveals Jesus' divine nature and His role in God's redemptive plan. This chapter will explore the significance of this miracle, delving into how it reveals Jesus' divinity and the deeper theological implications it holds.

The Context of the Miracle

The Wedding at Cana

The setting for this miracle is a wedding in Cana of Galilee. Weddings were significant social events in Jewish culture, often lasting several days. During such a celebration, running out of wine would have been a major social embarrassment for the host family. It is within this context of potential social crisis that Jesus performs His first miracle.

Jesus and His Mother

Mary, the mother of Jesus, brings the situation to His attention, saying, "They have no more wine" (John 2:3). Jesus' initial response, "Woman, why do you involve me? My hour has not yet come" (John 2:4), suggests a deliberate timing for His actions. Nevertheless, Mary instructs the servants, "Do whatever he tells you" (John 2:5), indicating her trust in His ability to resolve the issue.

The Miracle of Turning Water into Wine

The Act of Transformation

Jesus instructs the servants to fill six stone water jars with water. These jars, used for ceremonial washing, each hold twenty to thirty gallons. After filling the jars, Jesus tells them to draw some out and take it to the master of the banquet. When the master tastes the water that had been turned into wine, he is amazed, noting that it is of superior quality to what had been served earlier.

The Significance of the Miracle

This miracle is significant on multiple levels. Firstly, it demonstrates Jesus' divine authority over nature. The transformation of water into wine is an act of creation, showcasing Jesus' power to alter the fundamental properties of matter. Such a display of creative power points to His divine nature, echoing the creative acts of God in the Genesis account.

Secondly, the use of ceremonial jars for this miracle underscores a deeper spiritual transformation. These jars, associated with ritual purification, symbolize the old covenant and the Jewish purification rites. By transforming the water within them into wine, Jesus signifies the inauguration of a new covenant, where He Himself is the source of purification and joy.

The Revelation of Jesus' Glory

The Manifestation of Glory

John 2:11 states, "What Jesus did here in Cana of Galilee was the first of the signs through which he revealed his glory; and his disciples believed in him." This miracle is described as a sign, a term used throughout John's Gospel to indicate actions that reveal Jesus' divine glory and identity. The turning of water into wine is not merely a miraculous act but a revelation of Jesus' divine nature and glory.

The Disciples' Faith

The miracle at Cana leads to a deeper faith among Jesus' disciples. Witnessing this display of divine power and glory, they begin to understand more fully who Jesus is. This growing recognition of Jesus' divine nature is a central theme in John's Gospel, with each sign contributing to a deeper revelation of His identity as the Son of God.

Theological Implications of the Miracle

Divine Authority Over Nature

The miracle at Cana demonstrates Jesus' divine authority over nature. This authority is a key attribute of His divinity, highlighting His power to control and transform the natural world. Throughout the Gospels, Jesus' miracles often involve displays of power over nature, such as calming a storm, walking on water, and multiplying loaves and fishes. These acts reinforce His identity as the Creator and Sustainer of all things.

The New Covenant

The transformation of water into wine symbolizes the new covenant that Jesus inaugurates. Wine, often associated with joy and celebration in Jewish culture, here represents the abundant life and new relationship with God that Jesus offers. In the context of the wedding feast, the provision of the best wine at the end of the celebration signifies the surpassing greatness of the new covenant over the old.

In the Old Testament, wine is frequently used as a symbol of God's blessing and abundance (e.g., Psalm 104:15, Amos 9:13-14). By providing wine in such a miraculous manner, Jesus signals that He is the bringer of God's ultimate blessing and the fulfillment of Old Testament promises.

The Call to Faith

Recognizing Jesus' Divinity

The miracle at Cana calls believers to recognize Jesus' divinity and His role as the source of spiritual transformation and abundance. It challenges us to see beyond the miraculous act to the deeper spiritual reality it signifies. Recognizing Jesus as the one who has authority over nature and who inaugurates the new covenant invites us to place our faith in Him as the Son of God.

Responding with Obedience

Mary's instruction to the servants, "Do whatever he tells you," serves as a model for our response to Jesus. Faith in Jesus involves obedience to His commands and trust in His ability to provide and transform. Just as the servants obeyed Jesus' instructions and witnessed a miraculous transformation, we too are called to obey His word and experience His transformative power in our lives.

The Implications for Believers

Experiencing Transformation

Believing in Jesus as the one who transforms water into wine invites us to experience His transformative power in our lives. Just as He transformed the ordinary water into the finest wine, He can transform our ordinary lives into lives filled with His grace, joy, and purpose. This transformation is a hallmark of the new covenant, where believers are made new creations in Christ (2 Corinthians 5:17).

Sharing the Abundance

The abundance of wine provided by Jesus at the wedding feast symbolizes the overflowing blessings of the new covenant. As recipients of this abundance, believers are called to share the blessings of Christ with others. This involves proclaiming the good news of Jesus' transformative power and extending His grace and love to those around us.

Conclusion

John 2:1-11 reveals the profound truth of Jesus' divine nature through the miracle of turning water into wine. This miracle serves as a powerful sign that demonstrates His authority over nature and inaugurates the new covenant. By revealing His glory through this act, Jesus invites us to recognize His divinity and place our faith in Him as the Son of God.

As we embrace the significance of this miracle, we are called to respond with faith and obedience, trusting in Jesus' ability to transform our lives and provide for our deepest needs. This foundational truth shapes our identity as believers and empowers us to live out our faith with confidence and joy. Through Jesus, we encounter the divine source of life and transformation, leading us into a deeper relationship with God and a life of purpose and fulfillment.

This chapter challenges us to see the miracles of Jesus not merely as historical events but as signs that point to His divine nature and mission. By recognizing and responding to these signs, we deepen our faith and experience the abundant life that Jesus offers. This foundational truth shapes our identity as believers and calls us to share the hope and life we have found in Jesus with a world in need.

Jesus' Miracles as Signs of His Divinity

In John 4:46-54, we read about Jesus healing the nobleman's son. This miracle not only demonstrates Jesus' power over illness and life but also serves as a sign of His divine nature. This chapter will delve into the significance of this miracle, exploring how it reveals Jesus' divinity and the deeper theological implications it holds.

The Context of the Miracle

Jesus Returns to Cana

The setting for this miracle is Cana in Galilee, the same place where Jesus performed His first miracle of turning water into wine. John 4:46 says, "Once more he visited Cana in Galilee, where he had turned the water into wine. And there was a certain royal official whose son lay sick at Capernaum." The mention of Cana connects this miracle with Jesus' earlier demonstration of divine power, emphasizing the continuity of His ministry.

The Nobleman's Plea

A royal official, likely a man of significant status and influence, comes to Jesus in desperate need. His son is gravely ill in Capernaum, about twenty miles away. The nobleman implores Jesus to come and heal his son, showing his belief in Jesus' ability to perform miracles: "When this man heard that Jesus had arrived in Galilee from Judea, he went to him and begged him to come and heal his son, who was close to death" (John 4:47).

The Miracle of Healing

Jesus' Response

Jesus' initial response to the nobleman's plea is notable: "Unless you people see signs and wonders, you will never believe" (John 4:48). This statement addresses a broader issue of faith based on seeing miracles. Jesus challenges the nobleman, and by extension, all who seek signs, to have faith in His word and authority.

The Act of Healing

Despite the challenge, Jesus responds to the nobleman's persistent faith: "Go," Jesus replied, "your son will live" (John 4:50). The nobleman believes Jesus' word and departs. As he is on his way home, his servants meet him with the news that his son is alive and recovering. Upon inquiring about the time of his son's recovery, the nobleman realizes it coincides exactly with the moment Jesus declared, "Your son will live." This realization confirms the power of Jesus' word.

The Significance of the Miracle

Demonstration of Divine Authority

The healing of the nobleman's son demonstrates Jesus' divine authority over illness and life. Unlike other healings where Jesus physically touches or is present with the sick, this miracle is performed at a distance. Jesus speaks, and the boy is healed, illustrating His sovereign power over space and the physical world. This ability to heal with a word from a distance highlights Jesus' omnipotence and divine nature.

The Power of Jesus' Word

This miracle underscores the power and efficacy of Jesus' word. The nobleman's faith in Jesus' word, despite the physical distance, leads to his son's healing. This act of believing without seeing foreshadows the kind of faith Jesus calls for in all His followers. The emphasis on the power of Jesus' word aligns with John 1:1, where Jesus is identified as the Word, highlighting His divine nature and creative authority.

The Revelation of Jesus' Glory

Manifestation of Glory

John 4:54 states, "This was the second sign Jesus performed after coming from Judea to Galilee." The use of the term "sign" indicates that this miracle, like others, is a manifestation of Jesus' glory and divine identity. These signs are intended to reveal Jesus as the Messiah and Son of God, encouraging belief in Him.

The Nobleman's Faith

The miracle leads to a deepening of faith for the nobleman and his entire household: "So he and his whole household believed" (John 4:53). This response underscores the intended purpose of Jesus' signs—to bring people to faith in Him. The nobleman's progression from initial belief in Jesus' ability to perform miracles to a fuller faith in His identity as the divine Son of God serves as a model for all believers.

Theological Implications of the Miracle

Jesus' Authority Over Life and Death

The healing of the nobleman's son underscores Jesus' authority over life and death. His ability to heal a dying boy with a word signifies His power over the most fundamental aspects of human existence. This authority is a key attribute of Jesus' divinity, highlighting His role as the giver and sustainer of life.

Faith in Jesus' Word

This miracle emphasizes the importance of faith in Jesus' word. The nobleman's belief in Jesus' promise, despite not seeing the immediate result, exemplifies the kind of faith that is foundational to the Christian life. Jesus' word is powerful and trustworthy, and believers are called to place their faith in His promises.

The Call to Faith

Believing Without Seeing

The nobleman's faith challenges believers to trust in Jesus' word even when immediate evidence is not visible. This principle is echoed in John 20:29, where Jesus tells Thomas, "Blessed are those who have not seen and yet have believed." Faith based on Jesus' word, rather than on signs and wonders alone, is a deeper, more mature faith.

Responding to Jesus' Authority

Believers are called to respond to Jesus' demonstrated authority with trust and obedience. Recognizing His power over life and death invites a response of surrender and commitment to His lordship. This involves believing in His word, following His teachings, and living in accordance with His will.

The Implications for Believers

Trusting in Jesus' Power

The healing of the nobleman's son encourages believers to trust in Jesus' power to intervene in their lives. Whether facing illness, difficulty, or uncertainty, believers can have confidence in Jesus' authority and His ability to bring healing and restoration. This trust is rooted in His demonstrated power and His compassionate response to those who seek Him in faith.

Sharing the Testimony

The nobleman's testimony of his son's healing led to the faith of his entire household. Believers are called to share their testimonies of Jesus' work in their lives, encouraging others to place their faith in Him. By sharing how Jesus has intervened and brought healing or transformation, believers can help others recognize His divine nature and come to faith.

Conclusion

John 4:46-54 reveals the profound truth of Jesus' divine nature through the miracle of healing the nobleman's son. This miracle demonstrates His authority over illness and life, highlighting His omnipotence and the power of His word. As a sign, it reveals Jesus' glory and encourages faith in His identity as the Son of God.

Understanding this miracle deepens our faith and provides a foundation for trusting in Jesus' authority and power. It calls us to believe in His word, even when immediate evidence is not visible, and to respond to His authority with obedience and commitment. This foundational truth shapes our identity as believers and empowers us to live out our faith with confidence and joy.

Through Jesus, we encounter the divine source of life and healing, leading us into a deeper relationship with God and a life of purpose and fulfillment. This chapter challenges us to see the miracles of Jesus not merely as historical events but as signs that point to His divine nature and mission. By recognizing and responding to these signs, we deepen our faith and experience the abundant life that Jesus offers. This foundational truth shapes our identity as believers and calls us to share the hope and life we have found in Jesus with a world in need.

Jesus' Miracles as Signs of His Divinity

In John 5:1-15, Jesus heals a paralytic at the Pool of Bethesda. This miracle is significant not only because it demonstrates Jesus' compassion and power over physical ailments, but also because it illustrates His divine authority and ability to transform lives. By performing this miracle, Jesus reveals His divine nature and invites us to recognize Him as the source of healing and life. This chapter will explore the details of this miracle and its implications, delving into how it reveals Jesus' divinity and the deeper theological truths it conveys.

The Context of the Miracle

The Pool of Bethesda

The setting for this miracle is the Pool of Bethesda, located in Jerusalem near the Sheep Gate. The pool is described as having five covered colonnades and is a place where many disabled people used to lie—the blind, the lame, and the paralyzed. These people gathered at the pool in hope of being healed, as there was a belief that an angel would occasionally stir the waters, and the first person to enter the pool after this stirring would be healed.

The Paralytic's Condition

Among the disabled gathered at the pool is a man who had been paralyzed for thirty-eight years. His long-term condition highlights his desperation and hopelessness. When Jesus sees him lying there and learns of his condition, He asks, "Do you want to get well?" (John 5:6). This question, though seemingly obvious, is significant as it invites the man to express his desire for healing and engage with Jesus.

The Miracle of Healing

Jesus' Command

In response to Jesus' question, the paralytic explains his predicament: "Sir, I have no one to help me into the pool when the water is stirred. While I am trying to get in, someone else goes down ahead of me" (John 5:7). Jesus then issues a command that changes the man's life: "Get up! Pick up your mat and walk" (John 5:8). Immediately, the man is cured; he picks up his mat and walks.

Instant Healing

The instant nature of the healing is a testament to Jesus' divine power. The man, who had been paralyzed for nearly four decades, is immediately able to stand, walk, and carry his mat. This immediate transformation underscores Jesus' authority over physical ailments and His ability to bring about complete and instantaneous healing.

The Significance of the Miracle

Demonstration of Divine Authority

The healing at Bethesda is a clear demonstration of Jesus' divine authority over physical ailments. By commanding the paralytic to rise, Jesus shows that His words carry the power to heal and restore. This authority over physical conditions points to His divine nature and His role as the Creator who has power over the human body.

The Compassion of Jesus

Jesus' interaction with the paralytic also highlights His compassion. He approaches the man, initiates the conversation, and heals him without any prior request from the man. This act of compassion reflects Jesus' deep care for those who are suffering and His desire to bring healing and restoration to their lives.

The Revelation of Jesus' Glory

Manifestation of Glory

John 5:9 states, "At once the man was cured; he picked up his mat and walked. The day on which this took place was a Sabbath." This miracle, like others in John's Gospel, is described as a sign that reveals Jesus' glory. By performing this miracle, Jesus not only demonstrates His power but also reveals His identity as the Son of God who has come to bring healing and salvation.

The Sabbath Controversy

The fact that this miracle takes place on the Sabbath adds a significant dimension to its meaning. The Jewish leaders confront the healed man for carrying his mat on the Sabbath, which they consider a violation of the Sabbath law. When they learn that Jesus instructed him to do so, their focus shifts to Jesus, accusing Him of breaking the Sabbath.

Jesus' response to the Jewish leaders further reveals His divine nature: "My Father is always at his work to this very day, and I too am working" (John 5:17). By claiming that His work is aligned with the Father's ongoing work, Jesus asserts His divine authority and equality with God. This statement leads to increased opposition from the Jewish leaders, who recognize that Jesus is making Himself equal with God (John 5:18).

Theological Implications of the Miracle

Jesus' Authority Over Physical and Spiritual Realms

The healing of the paralytic demonstrates Jesus' authority over both the physical and spiritual realms. His ability to heal physical ailments points to His power over creation, while His teachings and actions reveal His authority in the spiritual realm. This dual authority underscores Jesus' divinity and His comprehensive role as the Savior.

The Offer of Spiritual Healing

While the miracle at Bethesda focuses on physical healing, it also points to the deeper spiritual healing that Jesus offers. After the healing, Jesus finds the man in the temple and warns him, "See, you are well again. Stop sinning or something worse may happen to you" (John 5:14). This warning highlights the connection between physical and spiritual well-being and underscores the importance of addressing the root cause of spiritual brokenness.

The Call to Faith

Recognizing Jesus' Divinity

The healing at Bethesda calls believers to recognize Jesus' divinity and His authority over all aspects of life. By acknowledging Jesus as the source of healing and restoration, we are invited to place our faith in Him and trust in His power to transform our lives.

Responding with Obedience

The paralytic's immediate response to Jesus' command serves as a model for our response to Jesus' authority. Faith in Jesus involves obedience to His commands and trust in His ability to bring about change. Just as the paralytic obeyed Jesus' command to get up and walk, we are called to respond to Jesus' words with faith and action.

The Implications for Believers

Experiencing Healing and Restoration

Believing in Jesus as the one who heals the paralytic invites us to experience His healing and restoration in our own lives. Whether facing physical ailments, emotional struggles, or spiritual brokenness, we can trust in Jesus' power to bring healing and renewal. This faith is rooted in His demonstrated authority and His compassionate desire to make us whole.

Sharing the Message of Healing

The healed paralytic's testimony to the Jewish leaders points to the importance of sharing our experiences of Jesus' work in our lives. As recipients of His healing and grace, we are called to testify to His power and invite others to encounter His transformative presence. By sharing our stories, we help others recognize Jesus' divinity and come to faith in Him.

Conclusion

John 5:1-15 reveals the profound truth of Jesus' divine nature through the miracle of healing the paralytic at Bethesda. This miracle demonstrates His authority over physical ailments, His compassionate care for those in need, and His identity as the Son of God. By performing this miracle, Jesus invites us to recognize His divinity and place our faith in Him as the source of healing and life.

As we embrace the significance of this miracle, we are called to respond with faith and obedience, trusting in Jesus' power to transform our lives and provide for our deepest needs. This foundational truth shapes our identity as believers and empowers us to live out our faith with confidence and joy. Through Jesus, we encounter the divine source of healing and restoration, leading us into a deeper relationship with God and a life of purpose and fulfillment.

This chapter challenges us to see the miracles of Jesus not merely as historical events but as signs that point to His divine nature and mission. By recognizing and responding to these signs, we deepen our faith and experience the abundant life that Jesus offers. This foundational truth shapes our identity as believers and calls us to share the hope and life we have found in Jesus with a world in need.

Jesus' Miracles as Signs of His Divinity

In John 6:1-14, we encounter one of Jesus' most well-known miracles: the feeding of the 5,000. This miracle is significant not only because of the sheer number of people fed but also because it showcases Jesus' divine provision and creative power. This chapter will explore the details of this miracle and its implications, delving into how it reveals Jesus' divinity and the deeper theological truths it conveys.

The Context of the Miracle

The Setting

The miracle takes place on the eastern shore of the Sea of Galilee. Jesus had crossed to this remote area with His disciples, and a large crowd followed Him because they had seen the signs He had performed by healing the sick. The crowd's persistence in following Jesus highlights their recognition of His extraordinary abilities and their hope to witness more of His miraculous works.

The Problem

As the day progresses, the crowd grows hungry, and the disciples express concern about how to feed such a large group. Jesus poses a question to Philip, "Where shall we buy bread for these people to eat?" (John 6:5). This question tests Philip's faith and sets the stage for the miraculous provision that follows.

The Miracle of Feeding the 5,000

The Offering

Andrew, another disciple, points out a boy with five barley loaves and two small fish but doubts their adequacy: "But how far will they go among so many?" (John 6:9). Despite the seemingly insignificant offering, Jesus takes the loaves and fish, gives thanks, and distributes them to the crowd.

The Multiplication

Jesus' act of giving thanks and distributing the loaves and fish results in a miraculous multiplication. The entire crowd of about 5,000 men, not counting women and children, is fed, and everyone eats as much as they want. After the meal, the disciples gather twelve baskets full of leftovers, underscoring the abundance of Jesus' provision.

The Significance of the Miracle

Demonstration of Divine Provision

The feeding of the 5,000 demonstrates Jesus' divine provision. In a situation where resources are scarce, Jesus provides abundantly for the physical needs of the crowd. This act of provision echoes God's provision for the Israelites in the wilderness when He supplied manna from heaven (Exodus 16). By performing this miracle, Jesus reveals Himself as the true provider who meets the needs of His people.

Creative Power

The miracle also showcases Jesus' creative power. He transforms a small amount of food into enough to feed thousands, highlighting His authority over the natural world. This creative power points to His divine nature as the Creator, who can bring forth abundance from scarcity. It echoes the creative work of God in Genesis, where God speaks creation into existence.

The Revelation of Jesus' Glory

Manifestation of Glory

John 6:14 states, "After the people saw the sign Jesus performed, they began to say, 'Surely this is the Prophet who is to come into the world.'" This miracle, like others in John's Gospel, is described as a sign that reveals Jesus' glory. By performing this miracle, Jesus not only demonstrates His power but also reveals His identity as the Messiah and Son of God.

The Disciples' Faith

The miracle leads to a deeper faith among Jesus' disciples. Witnessing this display of divine power and glory, they begin to understand more fully who Jesus is. This growing recognition of Jesus' divine nature is a central theme in John's Gospel, with each sign contributing to a deeper revelation of His identity as the Son of God.

Theological Implications of the Miracle

Jesus as the Bread of Life

Shortly after the feeding of the 5,000, Jesus explains the deeper spiritual significance of the miracle. In John 6:35, He declares, "I am the bread of life. Whoever comes to me will never go hungry, and whoever believes in me will never be thirsty." By providing physical bread, Jesus points to the greater truth that He is the spiritual sustenance for all who believe in Him.

The Abundance of God's Kingdom

The twelve baskets of leftovers collected after the feeding symbolize the abundance of God's provision. In God's kingdom, there is always more than enough to meet the needs of His people. This abundance contrasts with the scarcity mindset of the world and highlights the generosity and sufficiency of God's provision in Christ.

The Call to Faith

Recognizing Jesus' Divinity

The feeding of the 5,000 calls believers to recognize Jesus' divinity and His role as the provider of both physical and spiritual sustenance. By acknowledging Jesus as the source of all provision, we are invited to place our faith in Him and trust in His ability to meet our needs.

Responding with Gratitude

The miracle of feeding the 5,000 also calls us to respond with gratitude. Jesus' act of giving thanks before distributing the loaves and fish serves as a model for us. Recognizing God's provision in our lives should lead us to a posture of thankfulness and praise, acknowledging His generosity and care.

The Implications for Believers

Trusting in Jesus' Provision

Believing in Jesus as the one who feeds the 5,000 invites us to trust in His provision for our daily needs. Whether facing physical, emotional, or spiritual hunger, we can rely on Jesus' ability to provide abundantly. This trust is rooted in His demonstrated power and His compassionate desire to care for His people.

Sharing the Bread of Life

The miracle of feeding the 5,000 also calls believers to share the bread of life with others. As recipients of Jesus' provision, we are called to extend His generosity to those around us. This involves proclaiming the good news of Jesus' offer of eternal life and inviting others to come to Him for sustenance and satisfaction.

Conclusion

John 6:1-14 reveals the profound truth of Jesus' divine nature through the miracle of feeding the 5,000. This miracle demonstrates His provision and creative power, highlighting His authority over the natural world and His role as the provider of all needs. By performing this miracle, Jesus invites us to recognize His divinity and place our faith in Him as the source of both physical and spiritual sustenance.

As we embrace the significance of this miracle, we are called to respond with faith and gratitude, trusting in Jesus' ability to provide for our needs and recognizing His generosity in our lives. This foundational truth shapes our identity as believers and empowers us to live out our faith with confidence and joy.

Through Jesus, we encounter the divine source of provision and abundance, leading us into a deeper relationship with God and a life of purpose and fulfillment. This chapter challenges us to see the miracles of Jesus not merely as historical events but as signs that point to His divine nature and mission. By recognizing and responding to these signs, we deepen our faith and experience the abundant life that Jesus offers. This foundational truth shapes our identity as believers and calls us to share the hope and life we have found in Jesus with a world in need.

Jesus' Miracles as Signs of His Divinity

In John 9:1-12, we read about the miraculous healing of a man born blind. This miracle is significant because it not only showcases Jesus' power to give physical sight but also underscores His ability to grant spiritual sight. By performing this miracle, Jesus reveals His divine nature and highlights the deeper spiritual truths associated with His mission. This chapter will explore the details of this miracle and its implications, delving into how it reveals Jesus' divinity and the broader theological lessons it conveys.

The Context of the Miracle

The Setting

The miracle takes place as Jesus is passing by a man who has been blind from birth. The disciples question Jesus, asking, "Rabbi, who sinned, this man or his parents, that he was born blind?" (John 9:2). This question reflects the common belief at the time that physical ailments were directly linked to sin. Jesus' response redirects their thinking to a higher purpose.

Jesus' Purpose

Jesus replies, "Neither this man nor his parents sinned, but this happened so that the works of God might be displayed in him" (John 9:3). Jesus reframes the situation, indicating that the man's blindness serves a greater purpose: to reveal God's power and glory through His healing.

The Miracle of Healing

The Act of Healing

Jesus performs the miracle in a unique manner. He spits on the ground, makes mud with the saliva, and applies it to the man's eyes. He then instructs the man to go and wash in the Pool of Siloam. The man obeys, and upon washing, he gains his sight for the first time in his life.

The Significance of the Method

The method Jesus uses to heal the man is significant. The act of making mud with saliva and applying it to the man's eyes can be seen as a symbolic act of creation, reminiscent of God forming man from the dust of the ground in Genesis 2:7. This creative act underscores Jesus' divine nature and His authority as the Creator.

The Reaction to the Miracle

The Man's Testimony

After gaining his sight, the man returns home, and his neighbors and those who had seen him begging are astonished. They ask, "Isn't this the same man who used to sit and beg?" Some claim he is, while others insist he only looks like him. The man himself affirms, "I am the man" (John 9:9). He then recounts how Jesus healed him, testifying to the miracle he experienced.

The Pharisees' Investigation

The healing occurs on the Sabbath, which leads to controversy among the Pharisees. They investigate the miracle, questioning the man and his parents about how he received his sight. The Pharisees are divided, with some acknowledging the miracle and others condemning Jesus for performing it on the Sabbath.

The Theological Significance of the Miracle

Jesus as the Light of the World

Before healing the man, Jesus declares, "As long as I am in the world, I am the light of the world" (John 9:5). This statement is key to understanding the miracle's deeper meaning. Jesus' healing of the blind man is a physical demonstration of His role as the light who illuminates spiritual darkness. By granting physical sight, Jesus symbolizes the spiritual sight He offers to those who believe in Him.

The Power to Grant Spiritual Sight

The miracle underscores Jesus' ability to grant not only physical sight but also spiritual sight. The man born blind represents humanity's spiritual blindness. Jesus' act of healing serves as a sign that He is the one who can open the eyes of the spiritually blind, enabling them to see and understand the truth of God's kingdom.

The Revelation of Jesus' Glory

Manifestation of Glory

John 9:3 states that the man's blindness occurred so "that the works of God might be displayed in him." The miracle is a manifestation of Jesus' divine glory and power. By performing this miracle, Jesus reveals His identity as the Son of God and the one sent by the Father to bring light and life to the world.

The Man's Progressive Faith

The healed man's journey is also a story of progressive faith. Initially, he identifies Jesus as "the man called Jesus" (John 9:11). As he faces increasing opposition and interrogation, his understanding deepens, and he eventually acknowledges Jesus as a prophet (John 9:17). Finally, after Jesus reveals Himself as the Son of Man, the man responds with faith and worship, saying, "Lord, I believe," and he worships Him (John 9:38).

The Call to Faith

Recognizing Jesus' Divinity

The healing of the man born blind calls believers to recognize Jesus' divinity and His role as the light of the world. By acknowledging Jesus as the source of both physical and spiritual sight, we are invited to place our faith in Him and trust in His ability to illuminate our lives with His truth and grace.

Responding with Obedience

The man's obedience to Jesus' instruction to wash in the Pool of Siloam serves as a model for our response to Jesus' commands. Faith in Jesus involves trusting His word and acting on it, even when we do not fully understand the reasons. This obedience leads to transformation and a deeper understanding of who Jesus is.

The Implications for Believers

Experiencing Spiritual Sight

Believing in Jesus as the one who heals the blind invites us to experience spiritual sight. Jesus' ability to grant sight to the physically blind symbolizes His power to open our spiritual eyes, allowing us to see and understand the truth of God's kingdom. This spiritual sight transforms our lives, enabling us to live in the light of His presence and guidance.

Sharing the Light of Christ

The miracle of healing the blind man also calls believers to share the light of Christ with others. As recipients of Jesus' illumination, we are called to bear witness to His transformative power and invite others to come to Him for spiritual sight. This involves sharing our testimonies, proclaiming the gospel, and living as lights in a world darkened by sin and unbelief.

Conclusion

John 9:1-12 reveals the profound truth of Jesus' divine nature through the miracle of healing the man born blind. This miracle demonstrates His power to give both physical and spiritual sight, highlighting His role as the light of the world. By performing this miracle, Jesus invites us to recognize His divinity and place our faith in Him as the source of illumination and life.

As we embrace the significance of this miracle, we are called to respond with faith and obedience, trusting in Jesus' ability to transform our lives and provide spiritual sight. This foundational truth shapes our identity as believers and empowers us to live out our faith with confidence and joy.

Through Jesus, we encounter the divine source of light and truth, leading us into a deeper relationship with God and a life of purpose and fulfillment. This chapter challenges us to see the miracles of Jesus not merely as historical events but as signs that point to His divine nature and mission. By recognizing and responding to these signs, we deepen our faith and experience the abundant life that Jesus offers. This foundational truth shapes our identity as believers and calls us to share the hope and life we have found in Jesus with a world in need.

Jesus' Miracles as Signs of His Divinity

In John 11:1-44, we read about one of the most powerful and compelling miracles Jesus performed: the raising of Lazarus from the dead. This miracle is significant because it highlights Jesus' power over death and His role as the resurrection and the life. By performing this miracle, Jesus reveals His divine nature in a profound way, showcasing His authority over life and death. This chapter will explore the details of this miracle and its implications, delving into how it reveals Jesus' divinity and the deeper theological truths it conveys.

The Context of the Miracle

The Illness and Death of Lazarus

The story begins with the illness of Lazarus, the brother of Mary and Martha, who live in Bethany. The sisters send a message to Jesus, saying, "Lord, the one you love is sick" (John 11:3). Jesus' response to this news is intriguing: "This sickness will not end in death. No, it is for God's glory so that God's Son may be glorified through it" (John 11:4). Despite His love for Lazarus, Jesus delays His journey to Bethany, allowing Lazarus to die.

Jesus' Purpose

Jesus explains the purpose behind His delay to His disciples: "Lazarus is dead, and for your sake, I am glad I was not there, so that you may believe" (John 11:14-15). This statement indicates that the forthcoming miracle will serve a greater purpose in revealing Jesus' divine nature and strengthening the faith of His disciples.

The Arrival in Bethany

Martha's Faith

When Jesus finally arrives in Bethany, Lazarus has been in the tomb for four days. Martha goes out to meet Him and expresses her sorrow and faith: "Lord, if you had been here, my brother would not have died. But I know that even now God will give you whatever you ask" (John 11:21-22). Martha's statement reflects both her grief and her belief in Jesus' power.

Jesus' Declaration

Jesus responds with a profound declaration: "Your brother will rise again" (John 11:23). Martha misunderstands, thinking Jesus refers to the resurrection at the last day. Jesus clarifies, saying, "I am the resurrection and the life. The one who believes in me will live, even though they die; and whoever lives by believing in me will never die. Do you believe this?" (John 11:25-26). This declaration emphasizes Jesus' divine authority over life and death and His role as the source of eternal life.

The Miracle of Raising Lazarus

Jesus' Compassion

Mary, Lazarus' other sister, also meets Jesus, weeping. Jesus is deeply moved and troubled by the sorrow of Mary and the other mourners. He asks where Lazarus has been laid and weeps at the tomb (John 11:33-35). Jesus' tears reveal His deep compassion and empathy for human suffering, highlighting His fully human nature alongside His divinity.

The Command

At the tomb, Jesus orders the stone to be removed. Despite Martha's concern about the odor, Jesus reassures her: "Did I not tell you that if you believe, you will see the glory of God?" (John 11:40). After the stone is removed, Jesus prays, thanking the Father for hearing Him and stating that the miracle is for the benefit of the people, so they may believe that He is sent by God.

The Resurrection of Lazarus

Jesus then calls out in a loud voice, "Lazarus, come out!" (John 11:43). At His command, Lazarus emerges from the tomb, still wrapped in his burial clothes. Jesus instructs those present to take off the grave clothes and let him go (John 11:44). This miraculous act of raising Lazarus from the dead demonstrates Jesus' authority over death and His power to give life.

The Significance of the Miracle

Demonstration of Divine Authority

The raising of Lazarus is a clear demonstration of Jesus' divine authority over death. By calling Lazarus back to life with a command, Jesus reveals His power over the most final and irreversible human condition—death. This miracle confirms His identity as the Son of God, who holds authority over life and death.

Jesus as the Resurrection and the Life

Jesus' declaration, "I am the resurrection and the life," is central to understanding the significance of this miracle. He is not only the one who brings the dead back to life but also the very source of life itself. This statement underscores His divinity and His role in granting eternal life to all who believe in Him.

The Revelation of Jesus' Glory

Manifestation of Glory

John 11:4 and 40 highlight that the purpose of Lazarus' illness and subsequent resurrection is to reveal God's glory and the glory of the Son of God. The miracle serves as a powerful sign that reveals Jesus' divine nature and glorifies God through the manifestation of His power and authority.

The Impact on Believers

The miracle has a profound impact on those who witness it. Many of the Jews who had come to mourn with Mary and Martha believe in Jesus after seeing what He has done (John 11:45). This response underscores the purpose of the signs in John's Gospel: to lead people to faith in Jesus as the Messiah and the Son of God.

The Theological Implications of the Miracle

Jesus' Authority Over Death

The raising of Lazarus underscores Jesus' authority over death, the ultimate enemy of humanity. By demonstrating His power to raise the dead, Jesus provides a foretaste of His own resurrection and the promise of resurrection for all who believe in Him. This miracle assures believers that death is not the end, but that eternal life awaits them through faith in Christ.

The Promise of Eternal Life

Jesus' statement, "The one who believes in me will live, even though they die; and whoever lives by believing in me will never die," offers a profound promise of eternal life. This assurance of life beyond physical death is a central tenet of Christian faith, providing hope and comfort to believers.

The Call to Faith

Believing in Jesus' Divinity

The raising of Lazarus calls believers to recognize and believe in Jesus' divinity and His authority over life and death. By acknowledging Jesus as the resurrection and the life, we are invited to place our faith in Him and trust in His power to grant eternal life.

Responding with Obedience

Martha's and Mary's interactions with Jesus, as well as their obedience to His commands, serve as models for our response to Jesus' authority. Faith in Jesus involves trusting His words, acting on His instructions, and believing in His promises, even in the face of death.

The Implications for Believers

Hope in the Face of Death

The miracle of raising Lazarus provides believers with hope in the face of death. Jesus' authority over death assures us that physical death is not the final word. Through faith in Jesus, we have the promise of resurrection and eternal life, allowing us to face death with confidence and peace.

Living in the Light of the Resurrection

Believing in Jesus as the resurrection and the life calls us to live in the light of this truth. This involves living with the assurance of eternal life, sharing the hope of the resurrection with others, and living in a manner that reflects our faith in Jesus' power and promises.

Conclusion

John 11:1-44 reveals the profound truth of Jesus' divine nature through the miracle of raising Lazarus from the dead. This miracle demonstrates His authority over death and His role in the resurrection and life. By performing this miracle, Jesus invites us to recognize His divinity and place our faith in Him as the source of eternal life.

As we embrace the significance of this miracle, we are called to respond with faith and obedience, trusting in Jesus' ability to transform our lives and provide for our deepest needs. This foundational truth shapes our identity as believers and empowers us to live out our faith with confidence and joy.

Through Jesus, we encounter the divine source of life and resurrection, leading us into a deeper relationship with God and a life of purpose and fulfillment. This chapter challenges us to see the miracles of Jesus not merely as historical events but as signs that point to His divine nature and mission. By recognizing and responding to these signs, we deepen our faith and experience the abundant life that Jesus offers. This foundational truth shapes our identity as believers and calls us to share the hope and life we have found in Jesus with a world in need.

CHAPTER 11

JESUS' DEATH AND RESURRECTION

In John 19, we encounter the climactic moment of Jesus' earthly ministry: His crucifixion. This chapter captures the fulfillment of Scriptures, the demonstration of Jesus' sacrificial love, and the profound revelation of His divine nature. The events of Jesus' crucifixion and subsequent resurrection are central to Christian faith, highlighting His identity as the Son of God and His mission to redeem humanity. This chapter will explore the details of Jesus' death and resurrection, delving into how they reveal His divinity and the deeper theological truths they convey.

The Context of the Crucifixion

The Arrest and Trials

Before His crucifixion, Jesus is arrested in the Garden of Gethsemane and subjected to a series of trials before Jewish and Roman authorities. Despite being innocent, Jesus is falsely accused, mocked, and beaten. The Jewish leaders bring Jesus to Pontius Pilate, the Roman governor, demanding His crucifixion. Pilate, though finding no basis for a charge against Jesus, ultimately succumbs to the crowd's pressure and sentences Him to be crucified.

The Way to the Cross

Jesus is forced to carry His cross to Golgotha, the place of His execution. Along the way, He endures further mockery and physical abuse. The journey to Golgotha, also known as the Via Dolorosa, signifies Jesus' submission to the Father's will and His willingness to bear the weight of humanity's sin.

The Crucifixion

The Fulfillment of Scriptures

John's account of the crucifixion emphasizes the fulfillment of Old Testament prophecies. As Jesus is crucified, He is offered wine vinegar, fulfilling Psalm 69:21: "They put gall in my food and gave me vinegar for my thirst." The soldiers divide His garments and cast lots for His clothing, fulfilling Psalm 22:18: "They divide my clothes among them and cast lots for my garment." These fulfillments highlight the divine plan and Jesus' role as the Messiah foretold in the Scriptures.

The Inscription on the Cross

Pilate has an inscription placed above Jesus' head on the cross, reading "Jesus of Nazareth, the King of the Jews" (John 19:19). This inscription, written in Aramaic, Latin, and Greek, declares Jesus' identity to all who pass by. Although intended as a mockery, it inadvertently proclaims a profound truth: Jesus is indeed the King, not just of the Jews, but of all humanity.

The Demonstration of Sacrificial Love

Jesus' Words from the Cross

Jesus' statements from the cross reveal His profound love and concern for others, even in the midst of His suffering. He entrusts the care of His mother to the beloved disciple, saying, "Woman, here is your son," and to the disciple, "Here is your mother" (John 19:26-27). This act of compassion highlights Jesus' selfless love and care for His loved ones.

The Ultimate Sacrifice

Jesus' crucifixion is the ultimate demonstration of sacrificial love. As the Lamb of God, He willingly lays down His life to atone for the sins of the world. In John 15:13, Jesus says, "Greater love has no one than this: to lay down one's life for one's friends." By sacrificing Himself, Jesus fulfills this ultimate expression of love, offering redemption and reconciliation to humanity.

The Death of Jesus

"It is finished."

As Jesus nears the end of His earthly life, He declares, "It is finished" (John 19:30). This statement signifies the completion of His mission and the fulfillment of God's redemptive plan. Jesus has accomplished what He came to do: to bear the sins of the world and provide a way for humanity to be restored to a right relationship with God.

The Significance of His Death

Jesus' death is not just a tragic end but a victorious accomplishment. Through His death, Jesus conquers sin and death, providing the means for eternal life for all who believe in Him. His sacrificial death fulfills the requirements of divine justice and opens the way for God's grace and mercy to flow to all who accept His gift of salvation.

The Burial of Jesus

The Preparation and Burial

After Jesus' death, Joseph of Arimathea, a secret disciple of Jesus, asks Pilate for permission to take Jesus' body and bury it. Nicodemus, who previously visited Jesus at night, joins Joseph in preparing the body with spices and wrapping it in linen. They place Jesus' body in a new tomb in a garden near the crucifixion site (John 19:38-42). This act of love and respect fulfills the prophecy in Isaiah 53:9: "He was assigned a grave with the wicked, and with the rich in his death."

The Sealed Tomb

The tomb is sealed, and a stone is rolled over its entrance. This act signifies the finality of death and the hopelessness that the disciples and followers of Jesus feel. However, it also sets the stage for the miraculous event that will follow.

The Resurrection

The Empty Tomb

On the first day of the week, Mary Magdalene goes to the tomb and finds the stone rolled away and the tomb empty. She runs to tell Peter and the beloved disciple, who come and see the empty tomb for themselves. The grave clothes are left behind, and the linen that had been around Jesus' head is neatly folded (John 20:1-7). The empty tomb is the first sign of the resurrection, signaling that Jesus has conquered death.

Jesus' Appearances

Jesus begins to appear to His disciples, confirming His resurrection and transforming their despair into joy. He first appears to Mary Magdalene, who initially mistakes Him for the gardener. When Jesus calls her by name, she recognizes Him and proclaims, "I have seen the Lord!" (John 20:16-18). Jesus also appears to the disciples, showing them His wounds and giving them the Holy Spirit (John 20:19-22). His appearances provide undeniable proof of His resurrection and reinforce the disciples' faith.

The Theological Significance of the Resurrection

Victory Over Death

Jesus' resurrection is the ultimate demonstration of His divine nature and power. By rising from the dead, Jesus conquers death and demonstrates His authority over life and death. His victory provides the foundation for the Christian hope of eternal life and resurrection for all who believe in Him. As Paul writes in 1 Corinthians 15:20-22, "But Christ has indeed been raised from the dead, the first fruits of those who have fallen asleep. For since death came through a man, the resurrection of the dead comes also through a man. For as in Adam all die, so in Christ all will be made alive."

The Assurance of Salvation

The resurrection of Jesus provides assurance of salvation for believers. It confirms that Jesus' sacrificial death was sufficient to atone for sins and that His promise of eternal life is trustworthy. Romans 4:25 states, "He was delivered over to death for our sins and was raised to life for our justification." Through His resurrection, Jesus secures our justification and reconciliation with God.

The Call to Faith

Believing in the Risen Lord

The resurrection calls believers to place their faith in the risen Lord. Jesus' victory over death invites us to trust in His power to give us new life and to transform our lives. As Jesus said to Thomas, "Because you have seen me, you have believed; blessed are those who have not seen and yet have believed" (John 20:29). Faith in the resurrection is essential to the Christian life, providing the foundation for our hope and assurance.

Living in the Light of the Resurrection

Believing in the resurrection calls us to live in the light of this truth. This involves living with the assurance of eternal life, sharing the hope of the resurrection with others, and living in a manner that reflects our faith in Jesus' power and promises. It means embracing the new life that Jesus offers and allowing His resurrection power to transform us.

The Implications for Believers

Hope and Assurance

The resurrection of Jesus provides believers with hope and assurance. It assures us that death is not the end and that eternal life awaits us through faith in Christ. This hope allows us to face the trials and challenges of life with confidence and peace, knowing that our ultimate destiny is secure in Jesus.

Mission and Witness

The resurrection also calls believers to mission and witness. Just as Jesus commissioned His disciples to go and make disciples of all nations, we are called to share the good news of the resurrection with others. Our testimony to the risen Lord and our proclamation of His victory over death are central to our mission as followers of Jesus.

Conclusion

John 19 reveals the profound truth of Jesus' divine nature through His crucifixion and resurrection. These events demonstrate His sacrificial love, His fulfillment of the Scriptures, and His authority over life and death. By dying on the cross and rising from the dead, Jesus provides the means for our salvation and the assurance of eternal life.

As we embrace the significance of Jesus' death and resurrection, we are called to respond with faith and obedience, trusting in His power to transform our lives and provide for our deepest needs. This foundational truth shapes our identity as believers and empowers us to live out our faith with confidence and joy.

Through Jesus, we encounter the divine source of life and resurrection, leading us into a deeper relationship with God and a life of purpose and fulfillment. This chapter challenges us to see the crucifixion and resurrection of Jesus not merely as historical events but as signs that point to His divine nature and mission. By recognizing and responding to these signs, we deepen our faith and experience the abundant life that Jesus offers. This foundational truth shapes our identity as believers and calls us to share the hope and life we have found in Jesus with a world in need.

Jesus' Death and Resurrection

In John 20, we encounter the pivotal event of the Christian faith: the resurrection of Jesus Christ. This chapter captures the profound implications of Jesus' resurrection, demonstrating His victory over death and affirming His divine nature. The resurrection is not just a miraculous event; it is the cornerstone of Christian belief, revealing Jesus as the Son of God and the source of eternal life. This chapter will explore the details of Jesus' resurrection, delving into how it reveals His divinity and the deeper theological truths it conveys.

The Context of the Resurrection

The Empty Tomb

The narrative begins with Mary Magdalene visiting the tomb early on the first day of the week, only to find the stone removed and the tomb empty. She runs to inform Peter and the beloved disciple, who rush to the tomb and confirm her report. Inside, they find the linen cloths lying there, but Jesus' body is missing. The empty tomb is the first sign of the resurrection, indicating that something extraordinary has occurred.

Jesus' Appearances

Mary Magdalene's Encounter

After Peter and the beloved disciple leave, Mary remains at the tomb, weeping. She sees two angels sitting where Jesus' body had been and they ask her why she is crying. Turning around, she sees Jesus but does not recognize Him immediately. Thinking He is the gardener, she asks if He has taken Jesus' body. Jesus then calls her by name, "Mary." Recognizing His voice, she exclaims, "Rabboni!" (which means Teacher) (John 20:16). Jesus instructs her to go and tell His brothers that He is ascending to the Father. This encounter highlights the personal and transformative nature of the resurrection.

Jesus Appears to the Disciples

Later that day, Jesus appears to His disciples who are gathered behind locked doors out of fear. He greets them with "Peace be with you" and shows them His hands and side, confirming His identity and resurrection. The disciples are overjoyed. Jesus breathes on them, saying, "Receive the Holy Spirit" (John 20:22), commissioning them for their mission. This appearance underscores the reality of the resurrection and the empowerment of the disciples to continue Jesus' work.

Jesus and Thomas

One of the disciples, Thomas, was not present when Jesus first appeared to the group. When the others tell him about the resurrection, he expresses doubt, saying he needs to see and touch Jesus' wounds to believe. A week later, Jesus appears again and invites Thomas to put his finger in His wounds. Thomas responds with a profound confession of faith, "My Lord and my God!" (John 20:28). Jesus gently rebukes him, saying, "Because you have seen me, you have believed; blessed are those who have not seen and yet have believed" (John 20:29). This encounter highlights the importance of faith and the recognition of Jesus' divine nature.

The Theological Significance of the Resurrection

Victory Over Death

Jesus' resurrection is the ultimate demonstration of His divine nature and power. By rising from the dead, Jesus conquers death, the ultimate enemy of humanity. His victory over death provides the foundation for the Christian hope of eternal life and resurrection for all who believe in Him. As Paul writes in 1 Corinthians 15:54-57, "Death has been swallowed up in victory. Where, O death, is your victory?

Where, O death, is your sting?... But thanks be to God! He gives us the victory through our Lord Jesus Christ."

Affirmation of Jesus' Divinity

The resurrection affirms Jesus' divinity. By rising from the dead, Jesus proves that He is indeed the Son of God, as He claimed. This event validates His teachings, miracles, and His identity as the Messiah. Romans 1:4 states, "and who through the Spirit of holiness was appointed the Son of God in power by his resurrection from the dead: Jesus Christ our Lord." The resurrection serves as a divine seal of approval on Jesus' life and mission.

The Revelation of Jesus' Glory

Manifestation of Glory

The resurrection is a manifestation of Jesus' glory. It reveals His power over life and death and His role as the giver of eternal life. In His resurrection body, Jesus demonstrates the glorified state that believers will one day share. This glorification underscores His divine nature and the hope of glory for all who are united with Him.

The Impact on Believers

The resurrection has a profound impact on the lives of believers. It transforms their understanding of life and death, providing hope and assurance of eternal life. The disciples, once fearful and disheartened, become bold witnesses of the resurrection, empowered by the Holy Spirit. This transformation is a testament to the reality and power of the resurrection.

The Call to Faith

Believing Without Seeing

The story of Thomas highlights the importance of faith. Jesus blesses those who believe without seeing, emphasizing the value of trusting in Him based on the testimony of the Scriptures and the witness of the Holy Spirit. This call to faith is essential for all believers, inviting them to trust in the resurrection and the promises of Jesus.

Living in the Light of the Resurrection

Believing in the resurrection calls believers to live in the light of this truth. This involves living with the assurance of eternal life, sharing the hope of the resurrection with others, and living in a manner that reflects our faith in Jesus' power and promises. It means embracing the new life that Jesus offers and allowing His resurrection power to transform us.

The Implications for Believers

Hope and Assurance

The resurrection of Jesus provides believers with hope and assurance. It assures us that death is not the end and that eternal life awaits us through faith in Christ. This hope allows us to face the trials and challenges of life with confidence and peace, knowing that our ultimate destiny is secure in Jesus.

Mission and Witness

The resurrection also calls believers to mission and witness. Just as Jesus commissioned His disciples to go and make disciples of all nations, we are called to share the good news of the resurrection with others. Our testimony to the risen Lord and our proclamation of His victory over death are central to our mission as followers of Jesus.

Conclusion

John 20 reveals the profound truth of Jesus' divine nature through His resurrection. This event demonstrates His victory over death, affirms His divinity, and provides the foundation for the Christian hope of eternal life. By rising from the dead, Jesus invites us to recognize His divine nature and place our faith in Him as the source of eternal life.

As we embrace the significance of Jesus' resurrection, we are called to respond with faith and obedience, trusting in His power to transform our lives and provide for our deepest needs. This foundational truth shapes our identity as believers and empowers us to live out our faith with confidence and joy.

Through Jesus, we encounter the divine source of life and resurrection, leading us into a deeper relationship with

God and a life of purpose and fulfillment. This chapter challenges us to see the resurrection of Jesus not merely as a historical event but as a sign that points to His divine nature and mission. By recognizing and responding to this sign, we deepen our faith and experience the abundant life that Jesus offers. This foundational truth shapes our identity as believers and calls us to share the hope and life we have found in Jesus with a world in need.

CHAPTER 12

THE PURPOSE OF THE GOSPEL

In John 20:30-31, the author of the Gospel of John explicitly states the purpose of his writing: "Jesus performed many other signs in the presence of his disciples, which are not recorded in this book. But these are written that you may believe that Jesus is the Messiah, the Son of God, and that by believing you may have life in his name." These verses encapsulate the overarching goal of the Gospel—to lead readers to faith in Jesus as the Christ and the Son of God, and through that faith, to receive eternal life. This chapter will delve into these key points, exploring how they reveal Jesus' divine nature and the transformative power of belief in Him.

The Signs of Jesus

The Purpose of the Signs

Throughout the Gospel of John, various signs are recorded to demonstrate Jesus' divine nature and mission. These signs are not merely miracles but symbolic acts that reveal deeper spiritual truths about who Jesus is. John carefully selects these signs to build a compelling case for Jesus' identity as the Messiah and the Son of God.

Key Signs in John's Gospel

1. Turning Water into Wine (John 2:1-11): This first sign reveals Jesus' creative power and His ability to transform the ordinary into the extraordinary, symbolizing the new covenant He brings.

2. Healing the Nobleman's Son (John 4:46-54): This sign demonstrates Jesus' authority over illness and distance, emphasizing His divine power and compassion.

3. Healing the Paralytic at Bethesda (John 5:1-15): This miracle highlights Jesus' authority over physical ailments and His role as the healer.

4. Feeding the 5,000 (John 6:1-14): This sign underscores Jesus' provision and His role as the bread of life, who satisfies spiritual hunger.

5. Walking on Water (John 6:16-21): This miracle reveals Jesus' mastery over the natural world, showcasing His divine authority.

6. Healing the Man Born Blind (John 9:1-12): This sign emphasizes Jesus' power to give both physical and spiritual sight, illustrating His role as the light of the world.

7. Raising Lazarus from the Dead (John 11:1-44): This profound sign demonstrates Jesus' authority over life and death, affirming His identity as the resurrection and the life.

Believing that Jesus is the Christ, the Son of God

The Title "Christ"

The term "Christ" (Greek: Christos) means "anointed one" and is equivalent to the Hebrew term "Messiah." Throughout the Old Testament, the Messiah is prophesied as the one who will deliver and restore Israel. By identifying Jesus as the Christ, John asserts that Jesus fulfills these Messianic prophecies, bringing salvation not only to Israel but to the entire world.

The Title "Son of God"

Calling Jesus the "Son of God" highlights His unique relationship with God the Father. This title affirms Jesus' divinity, indicating that He shares the same nature as God. Throughout John's Gospel, Jesus' divine sonship is emphasized through His teachings, miracles, and His intimate relationship with the Father.

The Purpose of Belief

Faith Leading to Life

John's Gospel is written with the explicit purpose of leading readers to believe in Jesus as the Christ and the Son of God. This belief is not mere intellectual assent but a transformative faith that results in a relationship with Jesus and eternal life. John 3:16 succinctly captures this purpose: "For God so loved the world that he gave his one and only Son, that whoever believes in him shall not perish but have eternal life."

The Nature of Eternal Life

Eternal life, as presented in John's Gospel, is both a present reality and a future hope. It is the abundant life that begins the moment one believes in Jesus and continues forever in communion with God. John 17:3 defines eternal life as knowing the only true God and Jesus Christ, whom He has sent. This life is characterized by a deep, personal relationship with God, marked by love, joy, and peace.

The Transformative Power of Belief

Personal Transformation

Believing in Jesus leads to profound personal transformation. Throughout the Gospel, individuals who encounter Jesus and believe in Him experience significant changes in their lives. The Samaritan woman at the well, the man born blind, and Lazarus are just a few examples of lives transformed by faith in Jesus. This transformation is a testament to the life-giving power of Jesus and His ability to renew and restore.

Communal Transformation

Belief in Jesus also has communal implications. The early Christian community, formed by those who believed in Jesus, was characterized by love, unity, and mutual support. This transformative community is a reflection of the kingdom of God, where believers live out the values of the Gospel and bear witness to the love and grace of Jesus.

The Assurance of Faith

The Testimony of the Witnesses

John's Gospel provides a reliable testimony of those who witnessed Jesus' life, death, and resurrection. The signs and teachings recorded in the Gospel are corroborated by multiple witnesses, providing a solid foundation for faith. This eyewitness testimony assures readers of the truthfulness and reliability of the Gospel message.

The Role of the Holy Spirit

The Holy Spirit plays a crucial role in leading individuals to faith in Jesus. Jesus promises the coming of the Holy Spirit, who will guide believers into all truth, remind them of Jesus' teachings, and empower them to live out their faith (John 14:26, 16:13). The Holy Spirit's work in the lives of believers confirms their faith and assures them of their relationship with God.

The Call to Response

Invitation to Believe

The purpose statement in John 20:30-31 serves as an invitation to readers to believe in Jesus. It calls for a response of faith, encouraging individuals to place their trust in Jesus as the Christ and the Son of God. This invitation is open to all, offering the promise of eternal life to everyone who believes.

Living Out Belief

Believing in Jesus is not a one-time event but a lifelong journey. It involves growing in understanding, deepening one's relationship with God, and living out the implications of faith in daily life. This journey is marked by ongoing transformation, guided by the Holy Spirit, and grounded in the love and truth of Jesus.

Conclusion

John 20:30-31 encapsulates the purpose of the Gospel of John: to lead readers to believe that Jesus is the Christ, the Son of God, and that by believing, they may have life in His name. This purpose highlights the centrality of faith in Jesus, the transformative power of belief, and the assurance of eternal life.

As we embrace the purpose of John's Gospel, we are invited to respond with faith and commitment, recognizing Jesus' divine nature and trusting in His power to give us life. This foundational truth shapes our identity as believers and empowers us to live out our faith with confidence and joy.

Through Jesus, we encounter the divine source of life and salvation, leading us into a deeper relationship with God and a life of purpose and fulfillment. This chapter challenges us to see the Gospel of John not merely as a historical account but as a living testimony that invites us into a life-changing relationship with Jesus. By recognizing and responding to this invitation, we deepen our faith and experience the abundant life that Jesus offers. This foundational truth shapes our identity as believers and calls us to share the hope and life we have found in Jesus with a world in need.

APPENDIX A

KEY BIBLICAL PASSAGES REFERENCE

This appendix provides a compilation of key biblical passages referenced throughout the exploration of the Gospel of John, focusing on the divinity of Jesus Christ. These passages are foundational to understanding the theological insights and declarations made in John's Gospel regarding Jesus' divine nature and eternal existence.

John 1:1-3

"In the beginning was the Word, and the Word was with God, and the Word was God. He was with God in the beginning. Through him all things were made; without him nothing was made that has been made."

John 1:14

"The Word became flesh and made his dwelling among us. We have seen his glory, the glory of the one and only Son, who came from the Father, full of grace and truth."

John 2:1-11

"On the third day a wedding took place at Cana in Galilee. Jesus' mother was there, and Jesus and his disciples had also been invited to the wedding. When the wine was gone, Jesus' mother said to him, 'They have no more wine.' 'Woman, why do you involve me?' Jesus replied. 'My hour has not yet come.' His mother said to the servants, 'Do whatever he tells you.' Nearby stood six stone water jars, the kind used by the Jews for ceremonial washing, each holding from twenty to thirty gallons. Jesus said to the servants, 'Fill the jars with water'; so they filled them to the brim. Then he told them, 'Now draw some out and take it to the master of the banquet.' They did so, and the master of the banquet tasted the water that had been turned into wine. He did not realize where it had come from, though the servants who had drawn the water knew. Then he called the bridegroom aside and said, 'Everyone brings out the choice wine first and then the cheaper wine after the guests have had too much to drink; but you have saved the best till now.' What Jesus did here in Cana of Galilee was the first of the signs through which he revealed his glory; and his disciples believed in him."

John 4:46-54

"Once more he visited Cana in Galilee, where he had turned the water into wine. And there was a certain royal official whose son lay sick at Capernaum. When this man heard that Jesus had arrived in Galilee from Judea, he went to him and begged him to come and heal his son, who was close to death. 'Unless you people see signs and wonders,' Jesus told him, 'you will never believe.' The royal official said, 'Sir, come down before my child dies.' 'Go,' Jesus replied, 'your son will live.' The man took Jesus at his word and departed. While he was still on the way, his servants met him with the news that his boy was living. When he inquired as to the time when his son got better, they said to him, 'Yesterday, at one in the afternoon, the fever left him.' Then the father realized that this was the exact time at which Jesus had said to him, 'Your son will live.' So he and his whole household believed. This was the second sign Jesus performed after coming from Judea to Galilee."

John 5:1-15

"Some time later, Jesus went up to Jerusalem for one of the Jewish festivals. Now there is in Jerusalem near the Sheep Gate a pool, which in Aramaic is called Bethesda and which is surrounded by five covered colonnades. Here a great number of disabled people used to lie—the blind, the lame, the paralyzed. One who was there had been an invalid for thirty-eight years. When Jesus saw him lying there and learned that he had been in this condition for a long time, he asked him, 'Do you want to get well?' 'Sir,' the invalid replied, 'I have no one to help me into the pool when the water is stirred. While I am trying to get in, someone else goes down ahead of me.' Then Jesus said to him, 'Get up! Pick up your mat and walk.' At once the man was cured; he picked up his mat and walked. The day on which this took place was a Sabbath, and so the Jewish leaders said to the man who had been healed, 'It is the Sabbath; the law forbids you to carry your mat.' But he replied, 'The man who made me well said to me, "Pick up your mat and walk."' So they asked him, 'Who is this fellow who told you to pick it up and walk?' The man who was healed had no idea who it was, for Jesus had slipped away into the crowd that was there. Later Jesus found him at the temple and said to him, 'See, you are well again. Stop sinning or something worse may happen to you.' The man went away and told the Jewish leaders that it was Jesus who had made him well."

John 6:1-14

"Some time after this, Jesus crossed to the far shore of the Sea of Galilee (that is, the Sea of Tiberias), and a great crowd of people followed him because they saw the signs he had performed by healing the sick. Then Jesus went up on a mountainside and sat down with his disciples. The Jewish Passover Festival was near. When Jesus looked up and saw a great crowd coming toward him, he said to Philip, 'Where shall we buy bread for these people to eat?' He asked this only to test him, for he already had in mind what he was going to do. Philip answered him, 'It would take more than half a year's wages to buy enough bread for each one to have a bite!' Another of his disciples, Andrew, Simon Peter's brother, spoke up, 'Here is a boy with five small barley loaves and two small fish, but how far will they go among so many?' Jesus said, 'Have the people sit down.' There was plenty of grass in that place, and they sat down (about five thousand men were there). Jesus then took the loaves, gave thanks, and distributed to those who were seated as much as they wanted. He did the same with the fish. When they had all had enough to eat, he said to his disciples, 'Gather the pieces that are left over. Let nothing be wasted.' So they gathered them and filled twelve baskets with the pieces of the five barley loaves left over by those who had eaten. After the people saw the sign Jesus performed, they began to say, 'Surely this is the Prophet who is to come into the world.'"

John 6:16-21

"When evening came, his disciples went down to the lake, where they got into a boat and set off across the lake for Capernaum. By now it was dark, and Jesus had not yet joined them. A strong wind was blowing and the waters grew rough. When they had rowed about three or four miles, they saw Jesus approaching the boat, walking on the water; and they were frightened. But he said to them, 'It is I; don't be afraid.' Then they were willing to take him into the boat, and immediately the boat reached the shore where they were heading."

John 9:1-12

"As he went along, he saw a man blind from birth. His disciples asked him, 'Rabbi, who sinned, this man or his parents, that he was born blind?' 'Neither this man nor his parents sinned,' said Jesus, 'but this happened so that the works of God might be displayed in him. As long as it is day, we must do the works of him who sent me. Night is coming, when no one can work. While I am in the world, I am the light of the world.' After saying this, he spit on the ground, made some mud with the saliva, and put it on the man's eyes. 'Go,' he told him, 'wash in the Pool of Siloam' (this word means 'Sent'). So the man went and washed, and came home seeing. His neighbors and those who had formerly seen him begging asked, 'Isn't this the same man who used to sit and beg?' Some claimed that he was. Others said, 'No, he only looks like him.' But he himself insisted, 'I am the man.' 'How then were your eyes opened?' they asked. He replied, 'The man they call Jesus made some mud and put it on my eyes. He told me to go to Siloam and wash. So I went and washed, and then I could see.' 'Where is this man?' they asked him. 'I don't know,' he said."

John 11:1-44

"Now a man named Lazarus was sick. He was from Bethany, the village of Mary and her sister Martha. (This Mary, whose brother Lazarus now lay sick, was the same one who poured perfume on the Lord and wiped his feet with her hair.) So the sisters sent word to Jesus, 'Lord, the one you love is sick.' When he heard this, Jesus said, 'This sickness will not end in death. No, it is for God's glory so that God's Son may be glorified through it.' Now Jesus loved Martha and her sister and Lazarus. So when he heard that Lazarus was sick, he stayed where he was two more days, and then he said to his disciples, 'Let us go back to Judea.' 'But Rabbi,' they said, 'a short while ago the Jews there tried to stone you, and yet you are going back?' Jesus answered, 'Are there not twelve hours of daylight? Anyone who walks in the daytime will not stumble, for they see by this world's light. It is when a person walks at night

that they stumble, for they have no light.' After he had said this, he went on to tell them, 'Our friend Lazarus has fallen asleep; but I am going there to wake him up.' His disciples replied, 'Lord, if he sleeps, he will get better.' Jesus had been speaking of his death, but his disciples thought he meant natural sleep. So then he told them plainly, 'Lazarus is dead, and for your sake I am glad I was not there, so that you may believe. But let us go to him.' Then Thomas (also known as Didymus) said to the rest of the disciples, 'Let us also go, that we may die with him.' On his arrival, Jesus found that Lazarus had already been in the tomb for four days. Now Bethany was less than two miles from Jerusalem, and many Jews had come to Martha and Mary to comfort them in the loss of their brother. When Martha heard that Jesus was coming, she went out to meet him, but Mary stayed at home. 'Lord,' Martha said to Jesus, 'if you had been here, my brother would not have died. But I know that even now God will give you whatever you ask.' Jesus said to her, 'Your brother will rise again.' Martha answered, 'I know he will rise again in the resurrection at the last day.' Jesus said to her, 'I am the resurrection and the life. The one who believes in me will live, even though they die; and whoever lives by believing in me will never die. Do you believe this?' 'Yes, Lord,' she replied, 'I believe that you are the Messiah, the Son of God, who is to come into the world.' After she had said this, she went back and called her sister Mary aside. 'The Teacher is here,' she said, 'and is asking for you.' When Mary heard this, she got up quickly and went to him. Now Jesus had not yet entered the village, but was still at the place where Martha had met him. When the Jews who had been with Mary in the house, comforting her, noticed how quickly she got up and went out, they followed her, supposing she was going to the tomb to mourn there. When Mary reached the place where Jesus was and saw him, she fell at his feet and said, 'Lord, if you had been here, my brother would not have died.' When Jesus saw her weeping, and the Jews who had come along with her also weeping, he was deeply moved in spirit and troubled. 'Where have you laid him?' he asked. 'Come and see, Lord,' they replied. Jesus wept. Then the Jews said, 'See how he loved him!' But some of them said, 'Could not he who opened the eyes of the blind man have kept this man from dying?' Jesus, once more deeply moved, came to the tomb. It was a cave with a stone laid across the entrance. 'Take away the stone,' he said. 'But, Lord,' said Martha, the sister of the dead man, 'by this time there is a bad odor, for he has been there four days.' Then Jesus said, 'Did I not tell you that if you believe, you will see the glory of God?' So they took away the stone. Then Jesus looked up and said, 'Father, I thank you that you have heard me. I knew that you always hear me, but I said this for the benefit of the people standing here, that they may believe that you sent me.' When he had said this, Jesus called in a loud voice, 'Lazarus, come out!' The dead man came out, his hands and feet wrapped with strips of linen, and a cloth around his face. Jesus said to them, 'Take off the grave clothes and let him go.'"

John 19:16-30

"Finally Pilate handed him over to them to be crucified. So the soldiers took charge of Jesus. Carrying his own cross, he went out to the place of the Skull (which in Aramaic is called Golgotha). There they crucified him, and with him two others—one on each side and Jesus in the middle. Pilate had a notice prepared and fastened to the cross. It read: JESUS OF NAZARETH, THE KING OF THE JEWS. Many of the Jews read this sign, for the place where Jesus was crucified was near the city, and the sign was written in Aramaic, Latin and Greek. The chief priests of the Jews protested to Pilate, 'Do not write "The King of the Jews," but that this man claimed to be king of the Jews.' Pilate answered, 'What I have written, I have written.' When the soldiers crucified Jesus, they took his clothes, dividing them into four shares, one for each of them, with the undergarment remaining. This garment was seamless, woven in one piece from top to bottom. 'Let's not tear it,' they said to one another. 'Let's decide by lot who will get it.' This happened that the scripture might be fulfilled that said, 'They divided my clothes among them and cast lots for my garment.' So this is what the soldiers did. Near the cross of Jesus stood his mother, his mother's sister, Mary the wife of Clopas, and Mary Magdalene. When Jesus saw his mother there, and the disciple whom he loved standing nearby, he said to her, 'Woman, here is your son,' and to the disciple, 'Here is your mother.' From that time on, this disciple took her into his home. Later, knowing that everything had now been finished, and so that Scripture would be fulfilled, Jesus said, 'I am thirsty.' A jar of wine vinegar was there, so they soaked a sponge in it, put the sponge on a stalk of the hyssop plant, and lifted it to Jesus' lips. When he had received the drink, Jesus said, 'It is finished.' With that, he bowed his head and gave up his spirit."

John 20:1-18

"Early on the first day of the week, while it was still dark, Mary Magdalene went to the tomb and saw that the stone had been removed from the entrance. So she came running to Simon Peter and the other disciple, the one Jesus loved, and said, 'They have taken the Lord out of the tomb, and we don't know where they have put him!' So Peter and the other disciple started for the tomb. Both were running, but the other disciple outran Peter and reached the tomb first. He bent over and looked in at the strips of linen lying there but did not go in. Then Simon Peter came along behind him and went straight into the tomb. He saw the strips of linen lying there, as well as the cloth that had been wrapped around Jesus' head. The cloth was still lying in its place, separate from the linen. Finally the other disciple, who had reached the tomb first, also went inside. He saw and believed. (They still did not understand from Scripture that Jesus had to rise from the dead.) Then the disciples went back to where they were staying. Now Mary stood outside the tomb crying. As she wept, she bent over to look into the tomb and saw two angels in white, seated where Jesus' body had been, one at the head and the other at the foot. They asked her, 'Woman, why are you crying?' 'They have taken my Lord away,' she said, 'and I don't know where they have put him.' At this, she turned around and saw Jesus standing there, but she did not realize that it was Jesus. He asked her, 'Woman, why are you crying? Who is it you are looking for?' Thinking he was the gardener, she said, 'Sir, if you have carried him away, tell me where you have put him, and I will get him.' Jesus said to her, 'Mary.' She turned toward him and cried out in Aramaic, 'Rabboni!' (which means 'Teacher'). Jesus said, 'Do not hold on to me, for I have not yet ascended to the Father. Go instead to my brothers and tell them, "I am ascending to my Father and your Father, to my God and your God."' Mary Magdalene went to the disciples with the news: 'I have seen the Lord!' And she told them that he had said these things to her."

John 20:19-31

"On the evening of that first day of the week, when the disciples were together, with the doors locked for fear of the Jewish leaders, Jesus came and stood among them and said, 'Peace be with you!' After he said this, he showed them his hands and side. The disciples were overjoyed when they saw the Lord. Again Jesus said, 'Peace be with you! As the Father has sent me, I am sending you.' And with that he breathed on them and said, 'Receive the Holy Spirit. If you forgive anyone's sins, their sins are forgiven; if you do not forgive them, they are not forgiven.' Now Thomas (also known as Didymus), one of the Twelve, was not with the disciples when Jesus came. So the other disciples told him, 'We have seen the Lord!' But he said to them, 'Unless I see the nail marks in his hands and put my finger where the nails were, and put my hand into his side, I will not believe.' A week later his disciples were in the house again, and Thomas was with them. Though the doors were locked, Jesus came and stood among them and said, 'Peace be with you!' Then he said to Thomas, 'Put your finger here; see my hands. Reach out your hand and put it into my side. Stop doubting and believe

.' Thomas said to him, 'My Lord and my God!' Then Jesus told him, 'Because you have seen me, you have believed; blessed are those who have not seen and yet have believed.' Jesus performed many other signs in the presence of his disciples, which are not recorded in this book. But these are written that you may believe that Jesus is the Messiah, the Son of God, and that by believing you may have life in his name."

These key passages provide a comprehensive overview of the significant events and teachings in the Gospel of John that emphasize the divinity of Jesus Christ. Through these scriptures, readers can gain a deeper understanding of Jesus' identity, mission, and the eternal life offered through faith in Him.

APPENDIX B

GLOSSARY OF THEOLOGICAL TERMS

This glossary provides definitions of key theological terms referenced throughout the exploration of the Gospel of John. Understanding these terms will enhance comprehension of the theological insights and declarations made in the Gospel regarding Jesus' divine nature and eternal existence.

Atonement

Atonement refers to the reconciliation between God and humanity brought about by the sacrificial death of Jesus Christ. It involves the forgiveness of sins and the restoration of a right relationship with God.

Christ

Christ is the Greek equivalent of the Hebrew term "Messiah," meaning "anointed one." It is a title used to refer to Jesus, acknowledging Him as the one sent by God to save humanity and fulfill Old Testament prophecies.

Crucifixion

Crucifixion is the method of capital punishment in which a person is nailed or bound to a cross and left to die. It was the means by which Jesus was put to death, symbolizing His sacrificial love and atonement for the sins of the world.

Divine Nature

Divine Nature refers to the essential qualities and attributes that make up the being of God. In the context of Jesus, it signifies His divinity and equality with God the Father, as well as His eternal existence.

Eternal Life

Eternal Life is the gift of unending life in perfect fellowship with God, granted to those who believe in Jesus Christ. It is both a present reality and a future hope, encompassing a deep, personal relationship with God.

Faith

Faith is the confident trust in and reliance on God and His promises. In the context of the Gospel of John, it specifically refers to believing in Jesus as the Christ, the Son of God, and trusting in His ability to grant eternal life.

Incarnation

Incarnation is the Christian doctrine that the eternal Son of God took on human flesh in the person of Jesus Christ. It signifies God becoming fully human while remaining fully divine.

Logos

Logos is a Greek term meaning "Word." In the Gospel of John, it refers to Jesus as the pre-existent Word of God, through whom all things were created and who became flesh to reveal God's glory.

Messiah

Messiah is the Hebrew term for "anointed one." It refers to the promised deliverer and king prophesied in the Old Testament, fulfilled in the person of Jesus Christ.

Omnipotence

Omnipotence is the attribute of being all-powerful. It is a characteristic of God's divine nature, signifying His ability to do anything that is consistent with His character and will.

Omniscience

Omniscience is the attribute of being all-knowing. It is a characteristic of God's divine nature, indicating His complete and perfect knowledge of all things past, present, and future.

Resurrection

Resurrection refers to Jesus Christ's rising from the dead on the third day after His crucifixion. It is the foundational event of the Christian faith, demonstrating Jesus' victory over death and His divine nature.

Salvation

Salvation is the deliverance from sin and its consequences, granted by God's grace through faith in Jesus Christ. It involves forgiveness, reconciliation with God, and the promise of eternal life.

Sanctification

Sanctification is the process of being made holy, set apart for God's purposes. It involves the ongoing work of the Holy Spirit in a believer's life, transforming them into the likeness of Christ.

Son of God

Son of God is a title that affirms Jesus' unique relationship with God the Father, signifying His divinity and equality with God. It emphasizes His role in the Trinity and His participation in the creation and redemption of the world.

Trinity

Trinity is the Christian doctrine that God exists as three persons—Father, Son, and Holy Spirit—who are co-equal, co-eternal, and of one essence. It is a foundational concept for understanding the nature of God and the relationships within the Godhead.

Word (Logos)

Word (Logos) in the Gospel of John, refers to Jesus Christ as the pre-existent divine Word who became flesh to reveal God's truth and grace. It emphasizes His role in creation and His function as the ultimate revelation of God to humanity.

This glossary provides a foundational understanding of key theological terms that are crucial for grasping the depth of the Gospel of John's message about Jesus' divinity and eternal existence. Through these definitions, readers can better appreciate the profound theological insights presented in the Gospel.

APPENDIX C

FURTHER READING AND STUDY QUESTIONS

Further Reading

To deepen your understanding of the divinity of Jesus Christ as presented in the Gospel of John, consider exploring the following books and resources:

Books

1. "The Gospel of John: A Commentary" by Raymond E. Brown

- A comprehensive commentary that provides detailed insights into the text, historical context, and theological significance of the Gospel of John.

2. "Jesus According to Scripture: Restoring the Portrait from the Gospels" by Darrell L. Bock and Benjamin I. Simpson

- This book examines the portrayal of Jesus across the four Gospels, with a detailed analysis of John's unique presentation of Jesus' divinity.

3. "The Divinity of Jesus Christ: A New Testament Perspective" by Richard Bauckham

- An in-depth exploration of the New Testament's depiction of Jesus' divine nature, with a focus on John's Gospel.

4. "The Theology of the Gospel of John" by Dwight Moody Smith

- A scholarly work that delves into the theological themes and messages of John's Gospel, emphasizing the portrayal of Jesus as the Son of God.

5. "Encountering John: The Gospel in Historical, Literary, and Theological Perspective" by Andreas J. Köstenberger

- This book offers a well-rounded introduction to the Gospel of John, examining its historical context, literary structure, and theological themes.

Articles and Online Resources

1. "The Gospel of John" (BibleProject Video)

- A visual and narrative overview of the Gospel of John, highlighting its major themes and the portrayal of Jesus' divinity.

2. "The Deity of Christ in the Gospel of John" (Desiring God Article)

- An article that explores the various ways John's Gospel affirms the divinity of Jesus Christ.

3. "Understanding the Gospel of John" (Ligonier Ministries)

- A collection of articles and sermons that provide insights into the key themes and messages of the Gospel of John.

Study Questions

Use the following study questions to reflect on the themes and messages of the Gospel of John, particularly regarding the divinity of Jesus Christ:

1. John 1:1-3

- How does John's prologue establish the eternal nature and divinity of Jesus? What is the significance of referring to Jesus as the "Word"?

2. John 1:14

- What does the incarnation ("The Word became flesh") reveal about God's character and His plan for humanity?

3. John 2:1-11 (The Wedding at Cana)

- What does Jesus' first miracle at Cana reveal about His divine authority and His mission?

4. John 4:46-54 (Healing the Nobleman's Son)

- How does this miracle demonstrate Jesus' power over illness and distance? What does it teach us about faith?

5. John 5:1-15 (Healing the Paralytic)

- How does this healing on the Sabbath highlight Jesus' authority over physical ailments and religious traditions?

6. John 6:1-14 (Feeding the 5,000)

- What is the significance of Jesus providing physical sustenance to a large crowd? How does this sign point to His role as the bread of life?

7. John 6:16-21 (Walking on Water)

- What does Jesus walking on water reveal about His control over the natural world? How does this event reinforce His divine identity?

8. John 9:1-12 (Healing the Man Born Blind)

- How does the healing of the man born blind illustrate Jesus' ability to give both physical and spiritual sight?

9. John 11:1-44 (Raising Lazarus)

- What does the raising of Lazarus from the dead demonstrate about Jesus' power over life and death? How does this event prefigure His own resurrection?

10. John 19:16-30 (The Crucifixion)

- How does Jesus' crucifixion fulfill Old Testament prophecies and demonstrate His sacrificial love?

11. John 20:1-18 (The Resurrection)

- What is the significance of the empty tomb and Jesus' post-resurrection appearances? How do they confirm His victory over death and His divine nature?

12. John 20:30-31 (Purpose of the Gospel)

- How does the purpose statement in John 20:30-31 summarize the Gospel's message? Why is belief in Jesus as the Christ and the Son of God central to the Christian faith?

Conclusion

The Gospel of John provides a rich and profound exploration of the divinity of Jesus Christ, inviting readers to believe in Him as the Messiah and the Son of God. Through further reading and reflective study questions, you can deepen your understanding of this Gospel and its transformative message of faith and eternal life. As you engage with these resources and questions, may you grow in your knowledge of Jesus and experience the abundant life He offers.

BIBLIOGRAPHY

This bibliography provides a comprehensive list of sources and further reading materials that explore the divinity of Jesus in the New Testament and His connection to the Old Testament. These works include commentaries, theological studies, and scholarly articles that offer in-depth analysis and insights into the person and work of Jesus Christ.

Books

1. Bauckham, Richard. Jesus and the God of Israel: God Crucified and Other Studies on the New Testament's Christology of Divine Identity. Eerdmans, 2008.

   - A detailed examination of the New Testament's portrayal of Jesus' divine identity and its implications for early Christian theology.

2. Blomberg, Craig L. The Historical Reliability of John's Gospel: Issues and Commentary. IVP Academic, 2001.

- A scholarly defense of the historical reliability of the Gospel of John, with attention to its theological themes and presentation of Jesus.

3. Bock, Darrell L., and Benjamin I. Simpson. Jesus According to Scripture: Restoring the Portrait from the Gospels. Baker Academic, 2002.

- An analysis of the portrayal of Jesus across the four Gospels, with a focus on the unique presentation in John's Gospel.

4. Brown, Raymond E. The Gospel According to John (I-XII) and (XIII-XXI). Anchor Bible, 1966 and 1970.

- A comprehensive two-volume commentary on the Gospel of John, offering detailed exegetical and theological insights.

5. Carson, D.A. The Gospel According to John. Eerdmans, 1991.

- A thorough evangelical commentary on John's Gospel, addressing both historical and theological questions.

6. Keener, Craig S. The Gospel of John: A Commentary. Hendrickson Publishers, 2003.

- A comprehensive commentary that explores the historical context, literary features, and theological significance of John's Gospel.

7. Köstenberger, Andreas J. Encountering John: The Gospel in Historical, Literary, and Theological Perspective. Baker Academic, 1999.

- An introductory text that examines John's Gospel from multiple perspectives, including its theological themes.

8. Michaels, J. Ramsey. The Gospel of John. New International Commentary on the New Testament (NICNT), Eerdmans, 2010.

- A detailed and accessible commentary that provides insights into the theological message of John's Gospel.

9. Smith, Dwight Moody. The Theology of the Gospel of John. Cambridge University Press, 1995.

- A scholarly exploration of the major theological themes in the Gospel of John, focusing on its portrayal of Jesus.

10. Wright, N.T. The Resurrection of the Son of God. Fortress Press, 2003.

- An in-depth historical and theological study of the resurrection of Jesus, with significant attention to the Gospel of John.

Articles and Essays

1. Bauckham, Richard. "The Worship of Jesus in Early Christianity." Studies in Early Christology. T&T Clark, 1999, pp. 122-151.

- An article examining how early Christians worshipped Jesus and what this implies about their understanding of His divinity.

2. Hurtado, Larry W. "The Origin of the Devotion to Jesus." Journal of Theological Studies, vol. 50, no. 1, 1999, pp. 1-31.

- A scholarly article exploring the early Christian devotion to Jesus and its implications for understanding His divine status.

3. Lincoln, Andrew T. "The Beloved Disciple as Eyewitness and the Fourth Gospel as Witness." Journal for the Study of the New Testament, vol. 85, 2002, pp. 3-26.

- An article analyzing the role of the Beloved Disciple in John's Gospel and its implications for the Gospel's reliability and message.

4. Moloney, Francis J. "Signs and Shadows: Reading John 5-12." Interpretation, vol. 63, no. 4, 2009, pp. 354-366.

- An essay exploring the significance of the signs in John's Gospel and their theological implications.

Online Resources

1. BibleProject. "The Gospel of John." BibleProject Videos.

- A series of visual and narrative overviews of the Gospel of John, highlighting its major themes and theological messages.

- [BibleProject Video on John](https://bibleproject.com/explore/video/john/)

2. Desiring God. "The Deity of Christ in the Gospel of John." Desiring God Articles.

- An article exploring the various ways John's Gospel affirms the divinity of Jesus Christ.

- [Desiring God Article on John](https://www.desiringgod.org/articles/the-deity-of-christ-in-the-gospel-of-john)

3. Ligonier Ministries. "Understanding the Gospel of John." Ligonier Ministries.

- A collection of articles and sermons that provide insights into the key themes and messages of the Gospel of John.

- [Ligonier Ministries on John](https://www.ligonier.org/learn/series/gospel-of-john/)

Conclusion

This bibliography provides a comprehensive collection of resources for further study on the divinity of Jesus in the New Testament and His connection to the Old Testament. These materials offer valuable insights and in-depth analysis, enriching our understanding of the theological significance of Jesus Christ as presented in the Gospel of John. Through these works, readers can explore the profound and transformative message of John's Gospel, deepening their faith and knowledge of Jesus as the eternal Son of God.